DANISH ARCHITECTURE CENTRE
EXPERIENCES, INSPIRATION & DEVELOPMENT

ADDRESS
Danish Architecture Centre
Strandgade 27 B
1401 København K

WEB www.dac.dk
PHONE +45 3257 1930

The Danish Architecture Centre is a gathering point for everyone interested in architecture, urban development and innovation in the construction industry. Get updated through exhibitions and lectures given by Danish and international star architects; the web gallery; guided tours of Copenhagen's contemporary architecture; family workshops; and a wide variety of educational opportunities. If you want to explore things more deeply, the Danish Architecture Centre offers networking activities, professional events, debates etc. involving leading professionals in the fields of architecture, construction and urban development.

The Danish Architecture Centre puts the spotlight on how architecture, in the broadest sense, creates both cultural and economic value for people, businesses and communities by focusing on sustainable societal development from an economic, social, health and environmental point of view.

Visit the beautifully renovated warehouse right on the water's edge, and seek inspiration in Scandinavia's largest selection of Danish and international architecture and design books. In our Danish and international exhibitions current topics and trends are presented in the fields of architecture, construction and urban development. In the café on the 2nd floor you can enjoy brunch, lunch, something sweet, or just a cup of coffee with a direct view over the Copenhagen Harbour, the old Stock Exchange, the Opera House (03), the Royal Danish Playhouse (02), and the Inner Harbour Bridges (109).

Keep updated on **dac.dk** where you can also subscribe to our newsletter.

CONTENTS
BY THEME

CONTENTS
A–Z

CULTURE & LEISURE

KIM HERFORTH NIELSEN

Partner, 3XN

"IT STRENGTH-ENS OUR SELF-UNDER-STANDING"

Photo: Tuala Hjarnø

In Copenhagen, in just a few years, four major cultural institutions have been built, and the fifth is on its way. Recent years have also witnessed the emergence of several local cultural centres, of a kind we have never seen before. **"The buildings extend our thoughts about urban space,"** says Kim Herforth Nielsen, partner in the architectural firm 3XN, who were responsible for The Blue Planet, which opened at the beginning of 2013.

What significance do all these new cultural institutions have for the city?

"The major institutions testify to our self-understanding. They add character to places, and you can view them as a kind of manifestation of what sort of people we are. Generally, the new cultural institutions are singularly unpretentious. Although the Opera House (03) has its big dramatic eaves, and DR's concert hall (01) is clad in that strong blue colour, which no Danish architect would dream of using, the exteriors of these buildings make no big song and dance. Their interiors, on the other hand, are designed right down to the tiniest detail. There is a very strong correlation between outside and inside. If nothing else, they express a desire to make them welcoming in that very Danish, democratic way. The Royal Danish Playhouse (02) is particularly successful in this respect, because of the open lobby and promenade, which connects the house with the rest of the city."

What trends do we see in the cultural institutions?

"The design of the many local cultural centres plays with materials and design, perhaps as a consequence of the fact that many of the buildings have begun to serve several purposes: play, sports, cultural activities etc. It is also a consequence of the fact that many of the younger architects in Denmark have been heavily influenced by Dutch methods, which are extremely pragmatic. There is a strong emphasis on how sites should be used, and on how the building process should support interaction between people. And these notions about the functionality of urban spaces also affect our indoor spaces.

Compared to the major cultural institutions, we can probably trace this trend back to some kind of discretion. That is, if we disregard the Blue Planet. It is now not a new trend, but a form of self-understanding, which has exist-

ed in Danish architecture for a very long time. For the same reason, an iconic building such as The Blue Planet on Amager is a rarity. There is no tradition in Denmark for such an expressive building. But we have shifted slightly, thanks to the several international names, who have brought other traditions to this country: for example, Jean Nouvel with the DR Building. In architectural circles people are still inclined to look down their noses at buildings with powerful symbols. But in some cases it is the right thing to do. On Amager not so much is at stake, in architectural terms. There, it was necessary to give the Blue Planet its own power, which its whirling form has given it. With OMA's new building on the Bryghus site we will also see new rhythms. The fact that traffic is actually going to run right through the building, is something a Danish architect would probably never have dreamt of proposing."

In your opinion, in what way should the city improve its efforts?

"Architectural design is based on the sites, conditions and requirements which apply at any given time, so the focus should not simply be on the buildings themselves. Rather, it is the relations between the buildings we should assign even more attention to. The claim to a place is very significant, in terms of how it functions in the city. It is something you see a lot of good evidence of in relation to local cultural centres, which complement their surroundings beautifully."

What would you advise people to go and see?

"I would suggest that they go into the three different auditoria of the Copenhagen Opera House, the Royal Danish Playhouse and the DR Concert Hall. They are completely different. The Playhouse has a very special texture. It has an atmosphere of shadow and almost Nordic melancholy. The Copenhagen Opera House is warm in a different way, but much more spectacular with its huge installations. And when you enter the DR concert hall, you will experience a weird journey from the completely rough, cool lobby to the auditorium, which is like a big warm heart. And of course you have to get out and see the Blue Planet!"

01 KONCERTHUSET / DR BYEN

Emil Holms Kanal 20, København S

👤 CLIENT	DR Danish Broadcasting Corporation	
✎ ARCHITECT	Ateliers Jean Nouvel	
🔊 ACOUSTICS	Yasuhisa Toyota	
🔧 ENGINEER	NIRAS	
📅 TIME	Inaugurated in 2009	

They say that several musicians of the Danish National Symphony Orchestra had tears running down their cheeks, the first time they played in the main auditorium of Copenhagen's new concert hall. Along the way the building ran into many conflicts, but in 2009, when Jean Nouvel's multi-billion DKK building finally opened its doors, news of the event reverberated all the way to the *New York Times*, in which the architecture critic wrote that the building was one of the most beautiful he had seen in recent times.

Viewed from outside, the building does not draw a lot of attention to itself. However, at night, its simple façades, clad in blue textile, are brought to life with images projected on them. Behind the façade sits a giant meteor, a split second before it lands in an open field. That was the vision of the building's French star architect, who made this form a distinctive feature of the foyer. But this 'meteor', seemingly hovering in the air, is in fact a shell encasing the largest of the building's four auditoria.

The largest hall is unrivalled with its round, asymmetrical shape, undulating birchwood walls, staggered seating terraces and seats in various shades of red, which resemble the colour of the worn-out leather seats in the old concert hall.

The Japanese acoustician Yasuhisa Toyota was a key contributor to the design process. He created an exact scale model of the auditorium, in which tiny model figures were placed in the seats. Every single seat was tested, using special recording equipment, and the surroundings adjusted accordingly, to achieve optimal acoustics throughout the auditorium.

Photo: Peter Sørensen, CPH City & Port Development

Photo: Agnete Schlichtkrull

Koncerthuset also houses three smaller auditoria, each with its own distinctive design and specific acoustic solution. One auditorium is bright red and built for choirs. One is jet-black and reminiscent of a Steinway piano. The last is constructed with moveable wooden screens, on which Danish artists, who have played an important role in DR over the years, are portrayed in black.

Koncerthuset is the fourth and final segment in the *DR Byen* (DR City), which locates all of DR's production and TV and radio transmission in Ørestad. DR Byen is inspired by the concept of the kasbah, allowing easy access between the four segments. *Koncerthuset's* versatile programme, ranging from the great classical repertoire to rock concerts, award shows, and film events, is intended to generate a flow of life in the area and to attract as many different people as possible.

02 THE PLAYHOUSE

Sankt Annæ Plads 36, København K   E4

Photo: Jens Lindhe

Photo: Signe Baadsgaard

👤 CLIENT	The Royal Danish Theatre / Danish Ministry of Culture	
✎ ARCHITECT	Lundgaard & Tranberg Architects	
🔧 ENGINEER	COWI	
📅 TIME	Inaugurated in 2008	

The Royal Danish Playhouse is a stunning piece of architecture with an elegant exterior of warm wood, copper, glass, and narrow dark bricks, which were specially created for the Playhouse. The building projects out into the harbour and is surrounded by a promenade, which is supported by crooked Venetian columns, which plays a dual role, both as a jetty and a place to hang out in the summer. From here the audience is led into the open-plan café and restaurant and on to the Playhouse's three auditoria: *Store Scene* ('Main Stage'), *Portscenen*, and *Lille Scene*, which together can seat about 1,000 spectators. The audience can enjoy maximum comfort in the red theatre seats, which were sepcially designed for the Playhouse.

Uniting the whole building is an attic floor, which also serves as a canopy to shade the promenade and entrance. It is also where the dressing rooms, fitting rooms, wardrobe, offices, and cafeteria for actors and theatre staff are located. The glass façade provides a small glimpse backstage and glows with life and light, when darkness falls. In the middle of the building the fly tower reaches a height of 35 metres. Its copper-clad surface gleams in competition with the water in the harbour.

The location and function of the Royal Playhouse created an opportunity to incorporate a number of sustainable technical solutions. For example, seawater and excess heat from the hall are utilised to reduce energy consumption. A grant of DKK 5 m from the EU-funded Eco-Culture project helped to facilitate such solutions.

THE OPERA HOUSE

Ekvipagemestervej 10, København K

F3

Photo: Adam Mørk

👤 CLIENT	A. P. Møller og Hustru Chastine Mc-Kinney Møllers Fond til almene Formaal
✎ ARCHITECT	Henning Larsen Architects
🔧 ENGINEER	Rambøll / Ove Arup & Partners
📅 TIME	Inaugurated in 2005

Even from a distance, the Opera House stands out. with its central location and at the end of the historic axis running from the Marble Church to the very centre of the Main Stage. Visible from everywhere in the inner harbour, the Opera House's significant location stirred a particularly heated debate during the building's construction. Nevertheless, the classical music scene has been reinforced by 41,000 m², shared by 14 storeys, five of which are below water level.

While, viewed from a distance, the Opera House seems slightly fragmented, at close range its details become apparent. Upon arrival, the characteristic canopy sets the mood, drawing the audience into the magnificent foyer with its spectacular view of the harbour. The floor, walls, and staircases of the foyer are in light marble, in contrast to the core of the opera, which is a huge shell of golden maple. This is the location of the Main Auditorium, which can accommodate an audience of 1,400 people. In addition to the Main Auditorium, the Opera House also includes the *Takkelloftet* studio theatre, which can seat 180 people. This is a venue for experimental and multi-media projects.

A wonderful selection of Danish artists contributed to the décor of the Opera House. Per Kirkeby created four bronze reliefs for the foyer, while Olafur Eliasson designed the three lighting installations, which at night can be seen from the other side of the harbour. Per Arnoldi designed the front curtain for the Main Auditorium, and Tal R decorated the foyer of *Takkelloftet*.

04 THE ARCTIC RING

ZOO, Roskildevej 32, Frederiksberg B4

Photo: Bo Bøtther

CLIENT	Foreningen ZOO's Dyrefond
ARCHITECT	Dall & Lindhardtsen
ENGINEER	Strunge Jensen
TIME	Inaugurated in 2013

The polar bears frolic in this new Arctic landscape, where they can jump into the water from the specially placed rocks. The audience can dive in with the polar bears by going down a ramp into an acrylic tunnel. From here, you can clearly see the polar bears and seals swimming about, but happily a thick window separates the predators and the prey.

The Arctic Ring is made up of special geometric shapes: ellipses, curves and ramps cast in situ in white concrete. In some places the concrete was cast against acrylic sheets to achieve a glassy, 'ice-like' surface.

05 HIPPOPOTAMUS HOUSE

ZOO, Roskildevej 32, Frederiksberg B4

Photo: Jens Frederiksen

CLIENT	Foreningen ZOO's Dyrefond
ARCHITECT	Dall & Lindhardtsen
LANDSCAPE	Finn Jørsboe
ENGINEER	Rambøll
TIME	Inaugurated in 2007

Thanks to the full-height, armoured glass separating the hippo basin from the visitors' area, when the water is clear enough, you can see the hippos do their special slow motion underwater running on the bottom of the basin. The building is staggered towards the savannah area with large glass panes attracting light into the house, where there is enough room for larger birds to nest. The materials are stone, metal, and wood, the tone is warm, and the walls are cast in concrete reminiscent of the hippo's thick skin.

ELEPHANT HOUSE

ZOO, Roskildevej 32, Frederiksberg · B4

Photo: SLA

👤	CLIENT	Zoologisk Have København / Realdania / Agency for Palaces & Cultural Properties
✎	ARCHITECT	Foster + Partners
🌿	LANDSCAPE	SLA
🔧	ENGINEER	Rambøll
📅	TIME	Inaugurated in 2008

For some time the Zoo has made a concerted effort to improve animal welfare and provide better conditions for the visitors. Architects have contributed to the solution of this task with completely new ways of designing the animal facilities. The internationally renowned architect Norman Foster designed the new elephant house, circled by an outdoor landscape for the elephants and bordering *Frederiksberg Have*. There are no fences, only columns, moats, and walls of various heights to separate the elephants from the rest of the park.

Norman Foster has imprinted the elephant house with his distinctive hallmark. It consists of two gigantic glass domes, which are characteristic of his work. The glass domes make the building light and friendly, and a leaf pattern etched on to the glass filters the incoming light, giving an impression of trees and shrubbery. The overall goal of the building is to create the best possible conditions for the elephants: for example, by making the inner rooms big enough to allow the herd to stay together both day and night. Visitors can walk around the entire perimeter of the facility, across the elephants' indoor quarters, before continuing along the ramped promenade, which leads to the bottom level, where a number of interactive installations and exhibitions explain the history and biology of elephants.

You should allow yourself to experience the House from *Frederiksberg Have*, where you can get an excellent panoramic view of both the old and the new Elephant Houses. You might also be lucky enough to see the elephants playing in the mud alongside the waterholes.

07 BIBLIOTEKET

Rentemestervej 76, København NV

 B2

Photo: Adam Mørk

👤 CLIENT	City of Copenhagen
✎ ARCHITECT	COBE / TRANSFORM
🌱 LANDSCAPE	Schønherr
🔧 ENGINEER	Wessberg
📅 TIME	Inaugurated in 2011

The *Nordvest* district of Copenhagen has a new cultural beacon in the shape of the library. In 2009, there was a plan to merge the two local libraries and to extend the community centre. Instead a decision was made to combine all three and to create the cultural centre, which the area had been missing for a long time. The existing community centre was extended by 2,000 m², thus creating room for a large library, creative workshops, a café, citizens' advice bureau, meeting rooms, and local TV / radio. The result is the golden-coloured *Biblioteket* ('The Library') which, despite its name, contains much more than just metre upon metre of books. The name is actually more of a reference to the shape, which was inspired by a gigantic stack of books balanced on top of one another. The staggered 'books' are large, closely stacked buildings, while the spaces in-between are more open, transparent rooms with glass walls. The library is clad with expanded metal, creating a sensuous surface, on which the effect of light gives the building its golden appearance.

The architects designed not only the building but also the interior, which provides a fresh take on the issue of book storage. The children's library is shaped like a green and white climbing landscape, the young readers' library is silver, and the adult library is decorated like a cigar box with bookcases in light wood and dark leather armchairs.

The community centre, library, and the building's other facilities are linked together by walkways, staircases and staggered platforms across the foyer, which were decorated by well-known street artist *Husk Mit Navn*.

KORSGADEHALLEN

Korsgade 29, København N

📍 D3

Photo: Thomas Petri

👤 CLIENT	City of Copenhagen
✏️ ARCHITECT	BPP Arkitekter
🌿 LANDSCAPE	Henrik Jørgensen Landskab
🔧 ENGINEER	Lemming & Eriksson
📅 TIME	Inaugurated in 2006

Between *Korsgade* and *Åboulevarden*, a green, hilly landscape has sprouted out of the flat pavement. Under the grassy hill, you will find the *Korsgadehallen* sports and community centre which continues as an underground chamber below street level. This solution has provided the citizens of *Nørrebro* with an ultra-modern sports centre without having to relinquish the recreational green area, which was previously located here. You step into the house through a combined foyer and balcony. From there you move down to the courts, which are also used for theatre and music events.

ACTIVITY CENTRE

Vermundsgade 43A, København N

📍 C2

Photo: WITRAZ

👤 CLIENT	Lejerbo Aldersrogade
✏️ ARCHITECT	WITRAZ
🔧 ENGINEER	Wessberg
📅 TIME	Inaugurated in 2010

In the northwestern corner of Nørrebro, is a building whose façade resembles delicate cut-out paper. The building is a new community centre for sport and cultural events for the residents of *Den Grønne Trekant* ('The Green Triangle') housing complex, who for a long time lacked a place to gather. It is primarily used for after-school activities for the complex's 1,000+ children and young people, but there are also plans for adult amenities, including a big café on the ground floor. The building's striking façade is constructed from stamped aluminium sheets.

THE PRISM

Holmbladsgade 71, København S

F5

Photo: Torben Eskerod

Photo: Kontraframe

👤 CLIENT	City of Copenhagen / Foundation for Culture and Sport Facilities
✎ ARCHITECT	Dorte Mandrup Arkitekter / B&K+
🔧 ENGINEER	Jørgen Nielsen
📅 TIME	Inaugurated in 2006

In the summer of 2006, the area around *Holmbladsgade* in *Amager* finally got the sports facilities that the residents had been missing for years. The Prism is a result of the *Holmbladsgade* urban renewal, and has been given a central location which is connected to the park area in *Prags Boulevard* (33).

The sports and community centre is characterised by great flexibility, providing room for both organised and spontaneous sporting events. There will also be concerts and theatre in the building. The central architectural concept is a green indoor landscape undulating over several levels. Below is a large, green surface suitable for handball and other ballgames.

The green surface folds upwards at one end of the building towards a number of platforms with activities such as tai-chi or yoga. Under the platforms are changing rooms, offices and a café. The indoor landscape has a gigantic transparent cover, which stretches like a webbed skin between the new building and the four adjoining gables of an existing apartment building. This gives the sports and community centre its characteristic shape, while the transparent cover ensures an inflow of daylight throughout the building.

When darkness falls, The Prism is like a shining crystal in Holmbladsgade, and shadows from the indoor activities are visible from the outside.

ØRESUNDSVEJ 4-6

Øresundsvej 4-6, København S   📍 F5

Photo: Jens Lindhe

Photo: EFFEKT / WITRAZ

👤 CLIENT	City of Copenhagen
✎ ARCHITECT	Dorte Mandrup Arkitekter / WITRAZ / EFFEKT
🔧 ENGINEER	NIRAS / Jørgen Nielsen
📅 TIME	Inaugurated in 2013

The urban renewal of the area around *Øresundsvej* took place from 2005 to 2009. The focus was on culture, using existing institutions as a foundation. For many years, *Øresundsvej* was considered a thoroughfare with rundown housing and public spaces.

The main project is *Børnekulturhuset*, the new children's community centre. The house is the first of its kind in Denmark, created from the very beginning in collaboration with its future users. The house is designed for children, but also very much by children. For two years, the artist Kerstin Bergendal organised workshops, where the future users made drawings and models for the design of the house. At the corner, the main building is compressed to a height of one storey, in order to retain the view and the daylight in the courtyard behind. Inside, the building is designed with a number of staggered platforms and an open-plan entrance area, where the various rooms and functions of the building undulate up and down at various levels.

Another important project is *Musiktorvet*, a public space for music on the site of a former car park. The square is the link between the many cultural institutions, and creates a space for new outdoor cultural activities and urban living (markets, outdoor concerts etc.). The square is built around the concept of three stages in one common square.

The urban renewal also focuses on creating more green spaces, security and ambiance, all of which are reflected in large and small projects along the street and throughout the area.

12 MARITIME YOUTH CENTRE

Amager Strandvej 13, København S   📍 G5

Photo: Carsten Kring

👤 CLIENT	City of Copenhagen
✎ ARCHITECT	PLOT (BIG/JDS)
🔧 ENGINEER	ALECTIA
📅 TIME	Inaugurated in 2004

This youth centre with its characteristic undulating wooden deck is located in the Sundby Sailing Club's harbour at Amager Beach. Boats and other equipment are stored under the deck, and in the buildings there are club rooms, an office, a kitchen, and workshops. The deck itself is an area for play, barbecues and sunbathing. The problem of polluted soil has been elegantly and ingeniously solved by building the artificial landscape above the earth. The result is four times more outdoor space than originally planned and, of course, a beautiful and special building.

13 VALBY VANDKULTURHUS

Julius Andersens Vej 1A, København SV   📍 B6

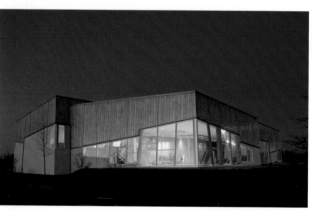

Photo: Jens Larsen

👤 CLIENT	City of Copenhagen
✎ ARCHITECT	Nøhr & Sigsgaard
🔧 ENGINEER	Rambøll
📅 TIME	Inaugurated in 2012

Anyone who loves exercise, wellness and playing in water will be in their element here. *Valby Vandkulturhus* does not look like an ordinary rectangular swimming pool. Slanted walls and asymmetrical lines are repeated inside and outside and create dynamic spaces, which challenge the senses and encourage people to have a great time. With *Valby Vandkulturhus* the architects actually succeeded in creating a low-energy swimming pool. In addition to innovative and energy-saving solutions in terms of lighting and insulation, heating is recycled from the litre upon litre of water, which flows through the showers every day.

BELLAHØJ AQUA ARENA

Bellahøjvej 1–3, Brønshøj

📍 B2

Photo: Kontraframe

👤 CLIENT	City of Copenhagen
🖊 ARCHITECT	Arkitema
🔧 ENGINEER	Søren Jensen / Balslev
📅 TIME	Inaugurated in 2010

The old open-air swimming pool in *Bellahøj* was originally designed in 1960 by the architect Tyge Hvass. Previously, because of the Danish climate, the open-air swimming pool was only open for swimming in the summer. The old swimming facility has now been renovated and extended and, when the new Bellahøj Aqua Arena opened in 2010, the former seasonal limitations were eliminated.

The original facility has been preserved, and the striking addition is the new indoor swimming pool, integrated into the original swimming pool and its landscape-like setting. It also provides a significant landmark, as one approaches the busy intersection. The new swimming facility is characterised in particular by the roof with an edge of opal glass. During the day the glass seems greenish, but when darkness falls. it lights up with changing colours.

The Bellahøj Aqua Arena is built in accordance with international competition standards, and includes pools for swimming, diving and teaching, as well as 1,000 seats for spectators. Changing the landscape has created space for more activities in the areas around the two existing open-air swimming pools.

Arkitema won the competition, which was organised by the City of Copenhagen, and the architecture practice based their design on the surrounding *Bellahøjhuse* and *Bellahøjparken*, so that the new facility would reflect the urban and natural features of the area. The Bellahøj Aqua Arena is used both as an ordinary swimming facility and for larger rallies and competitions.

15 THE BLUE PLANET

Jacob Fortlingsvej 1, Kastrup

H7

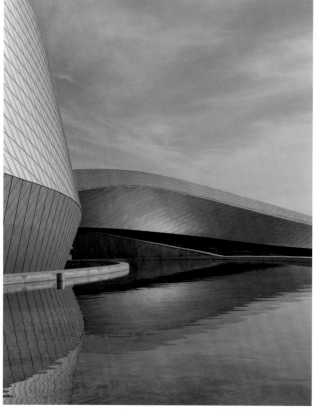

Photo: Bo Bolther

👤 CLIENT	Bygningsfonden Den Blå Planet (Realdania / Knud Højgaard Foundation / City of Tårnby)	
✎ ARCHITECT	3XN	
🔧 ENGINEER	Moe & Brødsgaard	
📅 TIME	Inaugurated in 2013	

Regardless of whether you arrive on land, by water, or from the air, it is difficult to overlook the new aquarium, *Den Blå Planet* ('The Blue Planet'). The building is spectacularly shaped like a giant whirlpool, a 'maelstrom', which engulfs visitors and gives them the feeling of being sucked down under the surface of the sea.

From the entrance, you proceed to the centre of the whirl, the round foyer. Here, you are literally under the sea, because the ceiling is made of glass and you look up through the bottom of a basin. Daylight is refracted by the water in the basin and creates a flickering of dots of light in the room, as if you were really under the sea.

From the foyer in the centre, five 'tentacles' radiate outwards, each one housing a different division of the aquarium and all kinds of exotic underwater creatures in cold, warm, salty and fresh surroundings. Each division has an entrance from the foyer, so you yourself choose your own direction through the Blue Planet.

The complex geometry and organic expression of the Blue Planet made it somewhat of a construction puzzle to build. The building consists of a steel frame, clad with sheets of aluminium, all with the same dimensions.

Covering an area of 9,000 m² and with aquarium technology which has to operate 24 hours a day, the Blue Planet is not exactly a leading light of sustainability. Nevertheless, the engineers have done their best to create solutions, which reduce energy consumption quite considerably: these include seawater cooling, insulation and low energy windows.

COPENHAGEN ARENA

Hannemanns Allé, København S

 E8

16

Renderings: 3XN / HKS

CULTURE & LEISURE

👤 CLIENT	Arena CPHX P/S
✎ ARCHITECT	3XN / HKS Architects
🔧 ENGINEER	Arup / ME Engineers
📅 TIME	To be inaugurated in 2015

In 2015, Copenhagen will get a new arena for large sports and cultural events. The arena will be built in Ørestad South. In addition to strengthening sports and cultural life in Copenhagen, the new arena will also play an important role in the urban development of Ørestad South, imbuing the area with life and attracting both tourists and international investments

The architecture of the arena consists of two primary elements: *Plinten* ('The Plinth') and *Hatten* ('The Hat'). The Plinth forms the base of the arena and contains a restaurant, a café, and other features, which open up towards the surrounding neighbourhood. The recesses of the Plinth are intended for use by the residents of the neighbourhood for activities such as markets and outdoor play, when there are no activities going on in the arena. The oval shape of the Hat floating above is clad with tiled slats, allowing passersby to glimpse the activities inside. The arena has permanent grandstands on three sides and a flexible fourth side, which can make room for a stage or another grandstand. There will be room for 12,500 spectators for sports events and up to 15,000 spectators for musical events. The space will also be flexible and scalable, making it possible to host events using only part of its capacity.

The master plan of the arena, designed by *Tegnestuen Vandkunsten*, proposes that the area will consist of a comparatively low building with a variety of architectural expressions. In the master plan, a park will link the new arena to the future school, ice-skating rink, and the district's childcare centre.

17 SPORTS HALL ON ARSENALØEN

Arsenalvej 6, København K   F4

Rendering: Christensen & Co. Arkitekter

👤 CLIENT	City of Copenhagen
✎ ARCHITECT	Christensen & Co. Arkitekter
🔧 ENGINEER	Rambøll
📅 TIME	To be inaugurated in 2013

For many years the residents of *Christianshavn* wanted a sports centre. Now they are getting one. It will be a centre with a focus on flexibility and sustainability. The ambition is for the striking red hall to serve as a community centre. Therefore, it will also have a large space in front on the canal with an outdoor café.

Indoors, the bright rooms will provide facilities for sporting activities, catering for individuals and small or large groups, and hosting cultural activities such as music, theatre shows, lectures, films, and meetings.

18 DANSEKAPELLET

Bispebjerg Torv 1, København NV   C1

Photo: Henning Sjøstrøm

👤 CLIENT	City of Copenhagen
✎ ARCHITECT	DOMUS Arkitekter
🔧 ENGINEER	Wissenberg
📅 TIME	Inaugurated in 2012

The chapel next to *Grundtvigskirken* in the *Nordvest* area was designed in 1908 as a last stop for the deceased. Today, the place has been converted to a spectacular 'dance chapel', creating life for the neighbourhood's children and young people. The solid walls of the chapel and load-bearing columns have been maintained, along with several of the old floors, while in the basement area an azure mosaic lights up the changing rooms where the former crematorium furnaces have now been replaced with shower stalls. *Dansekapellet* has two stages and three teaching studios.

BRYGHUSPROJEKTET

Christians Brygge, København K   E4

19

Renderings: OMA

CLIENT	Realdania / Realdania Byg	
ARCHITECT	Rem Koolhaas / OMA	
ENGINEER	COWI / Arup	
TIME	To be inaugurated in 2016	

When it is completed, the *Bryghusprojektet* will not only be an attraction in itself, but also transform the whole district by creating new settings for urban life and new life for the waterfront. The *Bryghusprojektet*, commissioned by Realdania, will be home to the Danish Architecture Centre, providing exhibition spaces, teaching and conference facilities, a café and bookshop. It will also contain apartments, offices, shops and a restaurant. The many different functions will be linked together by their location in the building's various staggered, transparent boxes which, throughout the building, will allow the users and their diverse activities to see and be seen. The concept of the architects was to create the atmosphere of a densely compact town within a single building. The façade of the building alternates greenish and white glass, with a distinctive green metal mesh.

One of the building's most remarkable elements is the connecting links, which will be created throughout the building. Christians Brygge, which is a relatively busy road, will run right through the building. Meanwhile pedestrians will be able to cross under the busy road. This underground passage will unite the city and the water and also include the entrance to the building.

Surrounding the building will be three different public spaces: a big urban plaza, a city park alongside the waterfront and a city playground, which will spread up the building on wide steps and terraces. The three different kinds of public space will encourage people to spend time here and generate activity in the area.

URBAN
SPACES

Photo: Søren Nordal Enevoldsen   Next spread: Kontraframe

TINA SAABY

Stadsarkitekt, Københavns Kommune

"WHEN YOU SAY THE WORD 'NATURE', IT ALWAYS BRINGS A SMILE TO PEOPLE'S FACES."

Photo: Ursula Bach

Copenhagen's public spaces are, more than ever before, the city's communal living rooms. "For many years, vibrant city life has been on the agenda, but in the future we will also require more quiet places," says Copenhagen city architect, Tina Saaby.

What significance do public spaces have for Copenhagen?

"Copenhagen's public spaces have, over the last few years, played a special role in the development of the city, is something we have heard time and time again. Since the start of this century, when the city entered a phase of enormous growth, there has been a strong focus on the life that goes on around buildings. Many people became aware of the great value which vibrant public spaces can, in all sorts of ways, provide: health, social diversity, security and interaction between people, to name but a few. The people of Copenhagen have acquired more leisure time, and their desire to use the city's public spaces has increased, as more and more opportunities have become visible to us. Today, the city's outdoor spaces can almost be regarded as our citizens' communal living rooms. They are effervescent in the summer, but also have a life of their own in the winter, without making any big song or dance.

This significance, which we attach to our public spaces in Copenhagen, finds expression in this axiom, which is part of our strategy for urban life: 'Urban life before public spaces. Public spaces before buildings.' There is very broad support for this idea throughout the city. Both at the political level and among large parts of the city's population, life around buildings is a very special issue, when it comes to the development of Copenhagen."

What are the latest trends in terms of public spaces?

"There have been several phases in the development of public spaces, but in general profound diversity has been the main hallmark of the development. This applies to the aesthetic, in which every single place assumes character from, and adds new character to, the area, where it is located. This applies to functionality. But it also applies to the flora and fauna to be found in the city. It is probably not many people who see it with the naked eye, but the city is a substantial shelter for biodiversity: insects, birds and bats, for example. Thus we should also

add that the green element plays a very prominent role in our organisation of public spaces. On one hand, this makes a positive contribution to the environment. On the other hand, it has a completely special, almost universally positive value for most people. When you say the word 'NATURE', it always brings a smile to people's faces."

In your opinion, what are we going to see more of in the future?

"The task of making the city even more climate-friendly will continue with the same high level of ambition as now. There will undoubtedly be more and more green areas in the city. New solutions for the development of the city include the diversion of large amounts of rainwater for recreational use. But mainly we will also expand our understanding of diversity more than ever before. This applies to the city's architecture, functions, lifestyles and atmospheres. We need room for more quiet places alongside the more vibrant places. That way we will definitely accommodate a wide variety of interests. We cannot expect everyone to be satisfied with every part of the city. We must be aware of this and make room for it."

What excursions would you recommend?

"Sønder Boulevard in Copenhagen is a wonderful place to experience how there really can be room for everything in one cohesive public space. Here you will meet both the old residents of the district, who still remember Vesterbro, when the neighbourhood was extremely poor, and the trendy young people and families, all of whom are making their mark on the area. The new islands out in Ørestad are also fantastic, with a completely new diversity, providing a multitude of walking routes with short cuts across the water. Their small scale adds a special something to Ørestad.

But the very best place is out in the Harbour Park at Bryggen. If you move a little further down towards the Bryggebro bridge, you can sit right underneath the quay and look out over the whole area, with Vesterbro in front of you and Bryggen just behind. It is a great place, from which to experience the city. I love sitting there completely alone, down by the water's edge in the middle of the big city."

20 FÆLLEDPARKEN

Fælledparken, København Ø

👤 CLIENT	City of Copenhagen	
✎ ARCHITECT	GHB Landskabsarkitekter / Nordarch / Bisgaard Landskab / Vilhelm Lauritzen / MLRP	
🔧 ENGINEER	Grontmij / SITE Design Group / Nielsen & Risager	
📅 TIME	Inaugurated in 2012	

Fælledparken's 11 million visitors each year make it the busiest park in Copenhagen. After many years as a military exercise facility, the early 1900s witnessed the area's conversion to a park. The intention was to give the people of Copenhagen a large outdoor space for sport and meetings. Since then the 58-hectare park has been used for everything from picnics, parties and exercise to concerts, car racing and relaxation.

Between 2008 and 2012 *Fælledparken* underwent the biggest park renovation in the history of Copenhagen. The park's facelift cost a total of DKK 196 m. However, despite the makeover, *Fælledparken* looks just the same as it always did. In order to maintain *Fælledparken's* unique character, all the new facilities were located at the outer edges of the park.

One of these spectacular new initiatives is the new 'Tower Playground', which comprises mini versions of five of Copenhagen's most famous towers. Apart from being pretty unusual, the playground is also a brilliant place for interactive play. With the latest technological backup, the playground is geared to extreme physical activity, and just a touch of competition. Children can go on electronic chases over the roofs of the Stock Exchange, solve a picture puzzle in the Round Tower or make political speeches from the top of the City Hall. The playground also adds to children's knowledge of the history of the city's iconic towers.

One of the best and biggest skate parks in northern Europe is another result of this large-scale renovation. In 2011 a 4,500 m² skateboard track, with a smooth, even concrete surface, took over the site of the old skate park.

Geared to the most up to date trends in the world of skating, the skate park is graded into three levels of difficulty, offering challenges for beginners, intermediates and champions!

Then, in 2012, the park's four football clubs were presented with the luxury of brand new changing facilities in the *Fælledparken* Club House. The architects from Vilhelm Lauritzen chose to submerge the building in the ground, using the surplus soil to create a small hilly area on the otherwise flat common. The hill has two functions. It shields the area against the noise of passing traffic and creates space around the building for relaxation or playing.

In addition to all the initiatives already mentioned, other improvements to the park include: 3.5 km of wider, illuminated jogging tracks, a bridge over *Fælledsø* ('The Commons Lake'), a flower garden, a 200 m² dance space, 152 benches, more than 1,000 new trees, fitness machines, beach volley ball courts, pétanque pitches and a new artificial grass pitch, where football players can run off some steam.

SQUARES OF FREDERIKSBERG

From Frederiksberg St. to Fasanvej St., Frederiksberg C4

Photo: Torben Petersen

CLIENT	City of Frederiksberg / Realdania
ARCHITECT	SLA
LIGHTING	Hansen & Henneberg
TIME	Inaugurated in 2005

As the result of a master plan, the public spaces between Frederiksberg's two central stations have been developed to provide easy connections, thus creating four different squares. Each one offers something different and has its own special character. Visitors to *Solbjerg Plads* can run around and play amongst hundreds of tiny puddles. What they are, in fact, is circular grooves in the paving stones, which collect rainwater. Meanwhile, thirty-two 'loudspeaker wells', located at various points around the square, transmit sound and play music.

A typical day on *Falkoner Plads* sees its wooden benches and multi-levelled steps bustling with students, visitors to the library, cinemagoers and fitness enthusiasts. Stroll over to *Fyrretræslunden* and you can laze on the grass, collapse on a bench, or stroll down the *Solbjergvej* pedestrian precinct next to the Frederiksberg Shopping Centre, maybe stopping to enjoy a cup of coffee in the shade of the big trees in front of the old station buildings.

Though each square has its own distinct hallmark, all four of them were inspired by the history of Frederiksberg as a garden town. That is why trees, bushes and stone pavements are vital elements in the design of all four squares. The squares change character according to the different rhythms of the hours and the seasons. At night the lighting changes and unites the various spaces, while during the day the squares are thoroughfares and meeting places for the wide variety of users. Even the plentiful rain, which the city is frequently subjected to, becomes an active element, enhancing the quality of the urban space and creating a variety of experiences.

SØNDER BOULEVARD

Sønder Boulevard, København V   D5

Photo: SLA

Photo: Troels Axelsen

URBAN SPACES

👤 CLIENT	City of Copenhagen
✎ ARCHITECT	SLA
💡 LIGHTING	Hansen & Henneberg / SLA
📅 TIME	Inaugurated in 2009

Vesterbro is an old working-class district, but over a number of years it has undergone a comprehensive clean-up programme and is now one of the most attractive places to live in Copenhagen. Today the district attracts young co-op owners and bar-goers out for a good time, while many families with children stay on, living in two apartments that have been knocked into one, with new, green courtyard areas. Old drying lofts have been converted into living spaces with high ceilings and roof terraces, while the streets are peppered with trendy shops and cafés.

Sønder Boulevard is probably the most outstanding example of this transformation process. Just a few years ago the street was christened, 'The biggest doggie toilet in Europe' and would have provided the perfect setting for an urban thriller. Now it is a lush green area, buzzing with the kind of life which many people feared would disappear into the green spaces behind the apartment buildings. An attractive combination of trees, pavements and grass has created a so-called 'park strip', which includes an herbaceous perennial garden, a toddlers' playground, a playing field, a BMX cycle area and seating areas, which provide a variety of environments. The road traffic, which used to be overwhelming, has been radically limited, and today you can happily picnic on the wide central reserve.

Families with children, teenagers and adults, who enjoy the occasional beer, now use the boulevard as if it were their very own front garden. However, despite all these radical changes, *Vesterbro* is still a very diverse district. On *Sønder Boulevard* the more fortunate house owners go about their business alongside the city's slightly more hardened customers.

23 NORDVESTPARKEN

At the intersection of Hulgårdsvej and Frederikssundsvej 📍 B2

Photo: Torben Petersen

👤 CLIENT	City of Copenhagen
🖊 LANDSCAPE	SLA
🔧 ENGINEER	Lemming & Eriksson
📅 TIME	Inaugurated in 2010

This 3.5-hectare area was formerly a garage facility for the city's buses. Today it has been transformed into a fairy-tale-like park, rich in sensuous impressions. Star-shaped seating islands, stripey street lamps, children's poems printed in the asphalt and sixty-three different species of tree from all over the world invite you on a voyage of discovery, while everything in the park is illuminated by the glow of beautiful and startling light effects. *Nordvestparken* is one of the few parks, which is at its most stunning at night. That is when its lighting universe really comes into its own.

24 MIMERSPARKEN

Tagensvej near Bispebjerg St., København N 📍 C2

Photo: Mahe Thing

👤 CLIENT	City of Copenhagen / Realdania
🖊 ARCHITECT	Peter Holst Landskab / Thing & Brandt Landskab
🔧 ENGINEER	Moe & Brødsgaard
📅 TIME	Inaugurated in 2012

In 2012 the deserted railway area between *Tagensvej* and *Mimersgade* was transformed into a welcomed green oasis in busy outer *Nørrebro*. There are facilities for every conceivable kind of sport: basketball, football, table tennis, roller hockey and lots more. Inspired by the former train tracks, the colourful climbing frame always scores top marks with the park's younger visitors. Barbecues and benches are ready for summer suppers, and the area is naturally abundant in apples, blackcurrants, cherry plums and wild strawberries.

BANANNA PARK

Nannasgade 6, København N   C2

Photo: Bjørn Djupvik

CLIENT	City of Copenhagen	
ARCHITECT	NORD Arkitekter	
LANDSCAPE	Schønherr	
TIME	Inaugurated in 2010	

Nørrebro's BaNanna Park represents a real success story. In 2004 local residents discovered that there were plans to build a housing estate on a grassy pocket of land on *Nannasgade*. This particular area was regularly used by local institutions as a necessary supplement to playgrounds and school yards. In fact, it was just about the only green space available in the *Mimersgade* neighbourhood. The staff of *Rådmandsgade* School, local parents and other passionate residents banded together and persuaded the City of Copenhagen to purchase the plot and to create BaNanna Park as part of the overall *Mimersgade* renewal project.

In spring 2010 the residents could at last set foot in their very own BaNanna Park. The Park is split up into three different areas: The Jungle, the Lawn and the Square. The Jungle consists of the trees that were already there plus some newly planted cherry-trees, which provide beautiful blossom in the spring. A handful of bamboo plants was also added to help create the right jungle-like density. The Lawn functions mainly as a playing field, but is also home to the characteristic banana-shaped mounds, which children can play on or spectators can sit on. The Square's spectacular, 14 m-high climbing arch marks the entrance to the Park. Here there is also a variety of outdoor furniture, encouraging visitors to spend some quality time in the Park.

The whole park is linked together by an asphalt loop, which is perfect for cycling or roller skating. There is lighting all the way along the path to rule out any possibility of dark, murky corners, while at night a couple of tall light poles with coloured light invest the Park with an almost fairy-tale atmosphere.

26 SUPERKILEN

Between Nørrebroparken and Tagensvej, København N 📍 C2

URBAN SPACES

Photos: Iwan Baan

👤 CLIENT	City of Copenhågen / Realdania
🖊 ARCHITECT	BIG / Topotek1
👁 ARTIST	SUPERFLEX
🔧 ENGINEER	Lemming & Eriksson
📅 TIME	Inaugurated in 2012

Superkilen ('The Super Wedge') is part of the overall facelift scheme for the *Mimersgade* district. This green wedge between *Tagensvej* and *Nørrebrogade* has been transformed into an activity precinct to encompass and enhance the cultural diversity of *Nørrebro*. *Superkilen* links the squares surrounding *Nørrebrohallen* with *Mimers Plads* and the Park precinct as far as *Tagensvej*, while the opposite side of *Nørrebrogade* connects with *Nørrebroparken*.

The project was conceived as a work-in-progress, so that residents and users could shape its ultimate identity. Indeed, since its inauguration, it has undergone a number of modifications, in terms of both paving and playground equipment. The inhabitants of *Nørrebro* come from fifty-seven different cultural backgrounds, a fact that has rubbed off on *Superkilen*, which is decorated with fifty-seven different objects, all suggested by the locals. These include a Japanese toy octopus and a Moroccan fountain.

Superkilen's multicultural space is subdivided into three different zones. The red zone (an extension of the *Nørrebrohallen* sports centre) was designed for team sports and outdoor fitness activities. The green park next to *Tagensvej* was landscaped with slopes, playing areas and picnic spots. The central black zone houses chess tables and benches for relaxation and meditation. At weekends a large portion of the 'Wedge' is turned into a bazaar for trade by local shopkeepers. *Superkilen's* final phase consists of a long cycle lane, running from the western end of *Frederiksberg* to *Nørrebro*. See also Green Cycle Routes (112) and *Åbuen* (111)

TORVEHALLERNE

Israels Plads, København K · D3

27

Photo: Arkitekturværkstedet v. Hans Peter Hagens

👤 CLIENT   Jeudan
✏️ ARCHITECT   Arkitekturværkstedet
                v. Hans Peter Hagens
🌿 LANDSCAPE   Jørn Palle Schmidt
🔧 ENGINEER   AI-gruppen
📅 TIME   Inaugurated in 2011

In 2011, after years of countless setbacks, Copenhagen finally saw the opening of a marketplace that would sell fresh produce in *Torvehallerne*, located at the northern end of *Israels Plads*. *Torvehallerne* consists of two market lanes, each covered by its own columned roof of zinc and cedar, with skylights running lengthwise. Taking inspiration from the Moorish Mezquita in Córdoba and the covered markets of southern Europe, the architects wished to provide a smooth transition between inside and outside, thus creating a delightful setting for shopping, meeting and eating.

ISRAELS PLADS SOUTH

Israels Plads, København K · D3

28

Rendering COBE

👤 CLIENT   City of Copenhagen
✏️ ARCHITECT   COBE / Birk Nielsen
🔧 ENGINEER   NIRAS
📅 TIME   To be inaugurated in 2014

If everything goes according to plan, the southern end of Israels Plads, which for many years has just been a derelict patch of asphalt, will be resurrected as a recreational link between the new *Nørreport Station*, *Ørstedsparken* and *Torvehallerne*. The creation of the new square will open up *Ørstedsparken*, which has always been blocked off from the city and its surroundings. The park's trees and green areas will literally step out on to *Israels Plads* and embrace the urban space with its pastoral setting. A stream will cross the square and lead into the park, where it will end in a small waterfall.

45

29 PLUG N PLAY

Asger Jorns Allé, København S E8

Photo: Kontraframe

👤 CLIENT	CPH City & Port Development
✎ ARCHITECT	Kragh & Berglund
👥 CONSULTING	Ørestad Urbane Haver /
	Parkour Team JiYo /
	Vesterbro Roller-skating Club
📅 TIME	2010–2014

The expression 'Plug n Play' was borrowed from the world of computers, but in *Ørestad South* it applies to urban living. The new activity area is a temporary provision intended to inject life into this rapidly growing new neighbourhood, in which large areas are presently under development. PLUG N PLAY will enable users to try out new forms of culture and sport. They can 'log in' to the various activities easily and with no obligation. There is everything anyone could wish for: from a speed skating track, a parkour course and an artificial turf football pitch to ball games, beach volley ball and a venue for markets and concerts. At one end of the facility there will be sixty urban allotments available for rent, where people can grow their own flowers and vegetables.

The grassy patches all over the area will act as small parks, where people can relax and watch the various sporting activities. There are also barbecue facilities adjacent to the allotments. Colourful containers have been installed throughout the area, where users can store their sports gear and garden tools, and there is access to water, power and toilet facilities. The plan is that, as *Ørestad South* continues to develop the most popular activities will remain or be relocated to other areas.

PLUG N PLAY is an excellent example of how, in recent years, temporary projects have been used as a means of urban planning, generating urban life during the process and creating value for residents, while development is under way. See also *Carlsberg* (125) and *A-huset* (60).

ØRESTAD URBAN PARK

Near Ørestads Boulevard 66, København S   📍 E7

30

Photo: Kontraframe

👤 CLIENT	Grundejerforeningen Ørestad City
✏️ ARCHITECT	MUTOPIA / GHB Landskabsarkitekter
👥 CONSULTING	Hausenberg / 2+1 Idébureau
📅 TIME	Inaugurated in 2008

The plans for Ørestad City included an immense park with minimal furnishing. As the inhabitants of the buildings moved in, they became the driving force in equipping the park according to their wishes. Today, the large park accommodates 8 minor 'islands' with distinct themes suitable for different kinds of leisure and games. When the excavations for the Metro City Ring (114) started, 100 tall trees that otherwise would have been cut down, were moved to the park in Ørestad. Beneath the park is a filtration system for road run-off, which is then redistributed out into the district's channels.

KASTRUP SEA BATHS

Amager Strandvej 301, Kastrup   📍 H6

31

Photo: Åke Eson Lindman

👤 CLIENT	Tårnby Council
✏️ ARCHITECT	White Arkitekter / White Design
🔧 ENGINEER	NIRAS
📅 TIME	Inaugurated in 2005

Kastrup Sea Baths rise out of the water like a conch shell. The facility was designed in the best materials, and is an outstanding blend of high quality and functionality. It is constructed in azobé wood, which is resistant to salt water. In the opinion of White Arkitekter, it was imperative to make the Sea Baths accessible to everyone. Therefore, the facility was designed to be handicap friendly. So, on one hand Kastrup Sea Baths provide swimmers with an excellent functional amenity, while, on the other, they create a beautiful, sculptural sight for anyone taking an evening walk.

AMAGER STRANDPARK

Amager Strandvej, København S

G5

Photo: Jan Kofod Winther

👤 CLIENT	Amager Strandpark I/S / City of Copenhagen / City of Frederiksberg / Copenhagen County	
✎ ARCHITECT	Hasløv & Kjærsgaard	
📅 TIME	Inaugurated in 2005	

Its extremely shallow water did not make the old Amager Beach the best place in the world for swimming. But now the addition of a 2 km-long artificial island, just a short distance out in the *Øresund*, has radically transformed that situation. Meanwhile, a long beach promenade with lagoons, paths and bridges has created life out there all year round. The new island has been split in two. While the northern part has a dune-like landscape, the southern part has the character of a park. Beautifully designed pedestrian and bicycle bridges cross over to the north and centre of the island, while in the southern section you can even drive over to the island. Happily, none of these changes have in any way destroyed the natural landscape or the view, the fresh air and salt water.

Light concrete beach stations have been placed along the promenade and function as open-air pit-stops. They house refreshment kiosks, toilets and other public amenities, while the roofs serve as vantage points, offering fantastic views of the large vessels sailing on the *Øresund*, the Øresund Bridge and the planes getting ready to land at Kastrup Airport. In the process of constructing *Amager Strandpark*, *Helgoland* (the old seawater swimming pool) was demolished. But it has now been reconstructed and is very popular with winter swimmers.

Just beyond the island and invisible to most visitors, there is also a diving facility, with artificial reefs, tunnels and an underwater statue. Meanwhile, *Øresundsvej* (11) and *Amager Strandvej* are witnessing the construction of modern town houses and tower blocks, some of which are fourteen-storey high.

PRAGS BOULEVARD

Prags Boulevard, København S   📍 F5

Photos Kontraframe

👤 CLIENT   City of Copenhagen
🖊 ARCHITECT   Kristine Jensens Tegnestue
🔧 ENGINEER   Moe & Brødsgaard
📅 TIME   Inaugurated in 2005

Prags Boulevard runs from *Amagerbrogade* and cuts through a number of residential districts and industrial areas, before culminating in a wonderful view of the *Øresund*. After the creation of *Amager Strandpark*, it seemed a logical next step to highlight *Prags Boulevard* as a vital link between town and water. The *Holmbladsgade* makeover provided a perfect opportunity, and the transformation turned out to be quite radical. Most of *Prags Boulevard* was closed to traffic, and green paths were created for the more vulnerable road-users, who can now walk or cycle all the way out to the beach, pretty much without disturbance.

The long park area of poplar trees and grass carpets form a 'green line', enhanced by specially designed chairs and street lamps in various shades of green. The whole boulevard is illuminated by these neon-green lamps, while the chairs are distributed at various points along the way. They can be moved around, so people can create their own personalised park areas and move the chairs into the sunshine. So far only very few of the chairs have disappeared; they are so heavy, that no one can manage to shift them more than a few metres!

This elongated urban space is sub-divided into seven different areas of activity, with such names as 'The Garden', 'The Stage', 'The Track' and 'The Box'. The Garden is a place to sit and relax amidst fragrant flowers and plants. The Stage is a place to play and perform on. Meanwhile, on the Track you can run about and mess around to your heart's content.

34 KALVEBOD WAVE

Kalvebod Brygge 1–5, København K   📍 E4

URBAN SPACES

Renderings: JDS / KLAR

👤 CLIENT	City of Copenhagen
✏️ ARCHITECT	JDS Architects / Klar Arkitekter
🔧 ENGINEER	Sloth Møller
📅 TIME	To be inaugurated in 2013

Ever since the construction of commercial domiciles and hotels on the waterfront at *Kalvebod Brygge* at the start of the '90s, the area has been notorious for its dull architecture and lack of urban life. All that is going to change, though, in the summer of 2013, when the multi-level, wave-shaped promenade is opened to the public.

The Wave will be an approx. 4000-m² promenade, constructed on two hundred and eighty-four piles. Its form will pull the promenade out into the sun, thus guaranteeing that *Kalvebod Brygge*, which is otherwise in the shade from noon onwards, gets as many hours of sunshine as possible. Two main areas will be constructed on the promenade. The northern area will serve as an oasis for relaxation, creating a kind of city-meets-maritime ambience. The southern area will be used for a variety of creative initiatives, including a small stage for music, parties, theatre and general entertainment. The Wave will also provide a jogging lane, various equipment for fitness and weight training, a canoe polo field and a canoe slide. There will also be a jetty for harbour buses, water taxis and sightseeing boats, at the same time offering mooring facilities for smaller vessels. The Wave will be built out of untreated, northern European oak, and all lighting will be LED.

Kalvebod Wave will provide the people of Copenhagen with a completely new harbour experience, right on their doorstep. The goal is to open up the area and reunite the city with the water. In addition to the Wave, a number of other projects have helped to breathe new life into the area. They include skater-friendly *'Skærgård' Park* next to SEB Bank & Pension (85) and *Under Krystallen*, a new public space with fountains, a reflecting pool and light art.

HARBOUR BATHS

Islands Brygge 14, København S   📍 E4

URBAN SPACES

👤 CLIENT	City of Copenhagen
✎ ARCHITECT	PLOT / BIG
🔧 ENGINEER	Birch & Krogboe
📅 TIME	Inaugurated in 2003 and 2013

In 2001, after many years of service as a conveyor belt for heavy ship traffic, the fairway was declared clean, and the first harbour swimming bath in years was opened to the public in 2003. It was so successful, that work soon started on the development of a permanent harbour swimming facility. The fledgling architecture practice PLOT (since divided into JDS and BIG) was entrusted with the task of designing a harbour swimming pool. The Harbour Baths have since become a permanent reference point in nearly all the city's debates on the subject of life by the water.

For seven days a week throughout the summer, there is room in the Harbour Baths for six hundred swimmers. The pool is rectangular, with long wooden walkways, which resemble the decks of a passenger ship. The diving tower looks like the prow of a ship and the lifeguard tower is like the ship's funnel. If the sun is shining, you can bet the pool will be crammed with people in an area that was formerly associated with heavy industry.

In 2011 the Harbour Baths opened their doors to winter swimmers, while 2013 will see the completion of a completely new extension, specially geared to those hardy winter vikings. BIG was responsible for designing the additions to the existing harbour baths. The boardwalk will be extended and raised to make space below for the saunas and thermal baths, which will have a fantastic view over the fairway. Inspired by the baths of ancient Rome, the floors will be decorated with mosaics by well-known street artist, *Husk Mit Navn*. The success of the baths opened the city's eyes to the harbour's strengths, and led to the creation of more harbour baths: at *Sluseholmen*, *Fisketorvet* and *Svanemøllen*.

36 VESTER VOLDGADE

Vester Voldgade, København V   📍 E4

Photo: GHB Landskabsarkitekter

👤 CLIENT	City of Copenhagen	
✎ ARCHITECT	COBE / GHB Landskabsarkitekter	
🔧 ENGINEER	Grontmij	
📅 TIME	Inaugurated in 2013	

Vester Voldgade has been resurrected as a green promenade for pedestrians, with a pavement that is wider on the sunny side of the street with room for hanging out and café life, while the road traffic is banished into the shade. This new-look street will link the city to the water, attracting life to the waterfront, where the future *Bryghusprojektet* (19) will be located. Rows of newly planted trees will restore the embankment to its former green character, and *Dantes Plads* and the square at *Vartov* by Hackett Hall McKnight Architects will be incorporated into the new public space.

37 HAUSER PLADS

Hauser Plads, København K   📍 E3

Photo: Ty Stange

👤 CLIENT	City of Copenhagen	
✎ ARCHITECT	K.B.P.EU – Karres en Brands & POLYFORM	
🔧 ENGINEER	Oluf Jørgensen	
📅 TIME	Inaugurated in 2013	

In 2009 the City of Copenhagen took the untraditional decision of creating a new work place beneath *Hauser Plads* for the city's Cleaning Facilities Centre (102). Thus a beautiful hole in the ground was created. Surrounding it is a fantastic new children's playground. The square and the hole are enclosed by a white slatted fence and lush pine trees. The surface is a mixture of real grass, artificial grass and granite on a rubber safety underlay. The design was the result of close discussion with local childcare centres to meet contemporary demands for a challenging playground.

KVÆSTHUSMOLEN PIER

Sankt Annæ Plads 36, København K   📍 E3

38

Rendering: Lundgaard & Tranberg Architects

👤 CLIENT	Kvæsthusselskabet
✏️ ARCHITECT	Lundgaard & Tranberg Architects
🔧 ENGINEER	COWI
📅 TIME	To be inaugurated in 2015

In 2004 the ferry to Oslo sailed out from *Kvæsthusmolen* quay for the very last time. Now this highly desirable plot could be looking at a very exciting future. In 2010 Ophelia Beach was created as an experiment. Based on their experience from this project, Lundgaard & Tranberg have embarked upon their plans for *Kvæsthusmolen*. The ambition is to create a wonderful space to be used day in and day out, and encouraging cultural life throughout the year. Seating steps at water level, pavilions and cafés, an outdoor stage and jetties for yachts, water taxis and sightseeing boats will bring *Kvæsthusmolen* back to life.

ØRESTAD ISLANDS

Along Sivegaden, København S   📍 E7

39

Photo: Anna Bisgaard Nøhr, ORT

👤 CLIENT	CPH City & Port Development
✏️ ARCHITECT	ORT – Open Research Team
🔧 ENGINEER	Aarsleff
📅 TIME	Inaugurated in 2012

The canal that runs alongside *Sivegaden* in Ørestad City has received a vital input in the shape of Ørestad Islands. The three circular, wooden constructions cross the canal, creating elegant thoroughfares, fun meeting points and fresh space for urban life. The islands are situated outside *VM Mountain* (41) *Lommeparken* and *Ørestad Gymnasium* (65). Each island possesses its own special focus and functions, but all three share the same basic concept: to create a space where the elements of play, culture and nature become an integral part of people's day-to-day lives.

HOUSING

Photo By & Havn. Next spread Jens Lindhe

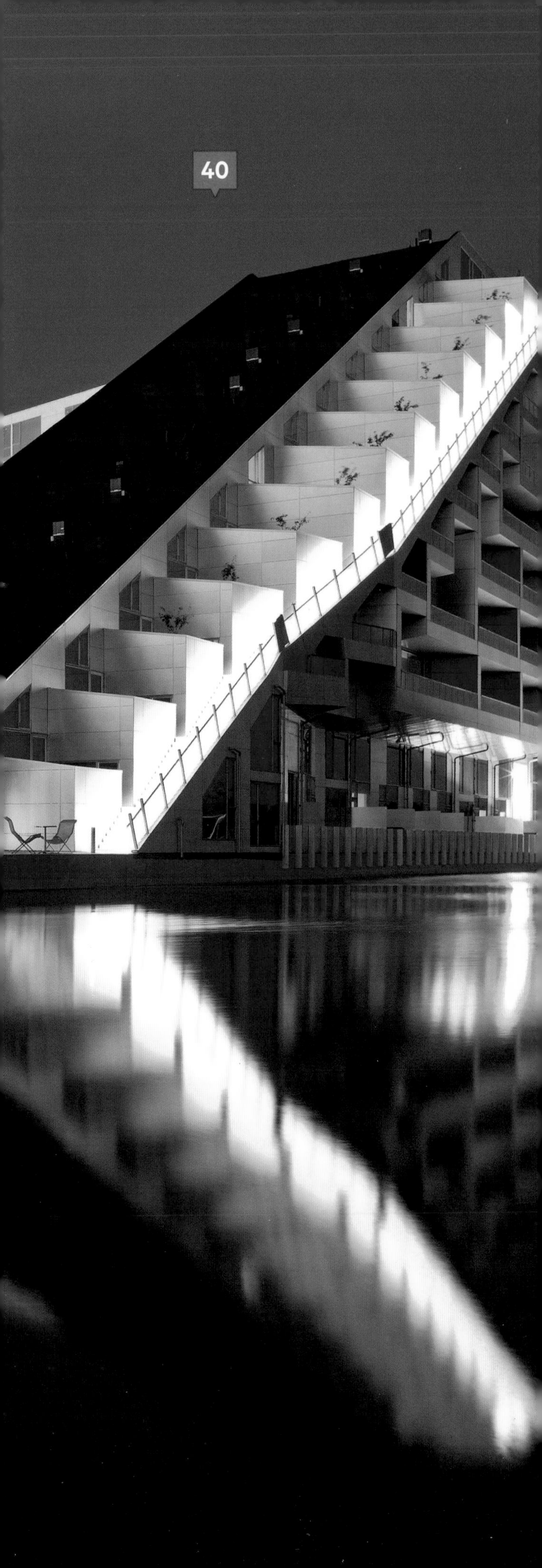
40

BENT MADSEN

Managing Director, BL – Danmarks Almene Boliger

"IT IS A KIND OF SOCIAL ENGINEERING"

Photo: Jørgen Jørgensen

Denmark has a long and strong tradition of building public housing with great architectural variety. "If we do not mix types of housing, we get both an unexciting and an unsafe city," says Bent Madsen, Managing Director of BL – Danmarks Almene Boliger.

Lots of new housing has been built in recent years. Why?

"The capital has been through a period of great growth, including many new large urban areas. More people are moving to the city. Families with children are more inclined to remain living here than earlier, plus we live longer. This has created a need for many new types of homes, that can meet the conditions. Public housing has played a particularly important role, because this type of housing is mixed with owner-occupied dwellings, so Copenhagen can continue to develop with the social balance and the diversity, which a good city needs. It is a kind of social engineering, which originates from a long Danish tradition of making space for diversity. Instead of people being grouped in enclosed enclaves, diverse types of people live next door to each other. This simply creates a greater feeling of safety in a city."

Are there new architectural trends in our contemporary house building?

"Most of the new housing developments have been designed by major Danish architects. But that is actually nothing new. The public sector has always been particularly enriched by famous Danish architects, who have worked with a strong focus on innovation and quality of building, based on the opportunities and the knowledge they had at the time. Today the expression of homes of course reflects our greatly increased energy awareness, which has also left its mark in the building materials. In newer construction the relationship between inside and outside has been given a new kind of attention. Entrances, openings to courtyards and special features on the ground floors will all help to create life around the buildings. The buildings blend with the surroundings outside the cadastre.

But the strongest trend is the way we mix dwellings today. Previously we built public housing in very large

units. This does not work optimally in today's society, where in many places areas have evolved in a closed-off and uniform way, diametrically opposed to their intentions. In the public housing we build today, there are a maximum of 30 public dwellings in one unit. They are also located right next to other types of housing (cooperatives and owner-occupied apartments). Actually, there are several examples of new housing, where several types of housing share a single roof. If we do not mix housing types as much as possible, we get both an unexciting and an unsafe city, where we run the risk of not creating room for the diversity, which is so important for our society."

What is the next thing we are going to see?

"We will continue to build new housing developments. Several new urban areas are in the pipeline, which will also provide people with a good standard of living. We live longer today, so there is also a need for more housing for the elderly. At the same time, we will see even more environmental makeovers of the older residential areas. We will also definitely see brand new architectural expression in the future, reflecting the major development of new technological environmental campaigns and construction methods. Maybe our homes will look completely different, in ways we cannot even imagine now."

What would you recommend people to go and see?

"I would suggest a trip to *Sømærk* (58) at *Teglholmen* (129). The project has created an environment which is very vibrant, and where water is used in an interesting way by many different people. A trip to Ørestad City is also interesting. Just to experience the enormous scale of the various types of housing."

8HOUSE

Richard Mortensens Vej 61, København S

👤 CLIENT	Dansk Olie Kompagni / Høpfner / Ejendomsselskabet St. Frederikslund	
✎ ARCHITECT	BIG	
🔧 ENGINEER	Moe & Brødsgaard	
📅 TIME	Inaugurated in 2010	

At the outermost tip of *Ørestad* stands a spectacular building. Actually it is more like a whole village in itself. The intention of the project was to generate urban living within the site itself, instead of relying on the presumption that urban life would only be evident in the streets between *Ørestad's* various sites. The form of the building is based on the classic block concept. But it is 'twisted' in the middle and 'squashed' at the end, which faces the attractive light, air and view of the expansive common.

Commercial premises and childcare facilities are located at street level, close to the essential customers and with extra space available in the darker parts of the building. On the upper floors the residential units are garlanded along a line, which winds its way round in a figure-of-eight, before ending in airy penthouse apartments at the very top.

The 476 residential units include apartments with balconies, duplex 'townhouses' and the penthouses at the top of the building – the exclusive end of the 'village'. The whole building is tied together by a path, which winds its way 1.5 kilometres up, round, past and through the rows of homes. This public path – '8House Street' – has a zigzag-patterned surface, which is said to help wheelchair-users tilt their chairs at the right angle, as they move along the often steep street.

The many different types of residence cater for many different types of family. However, the highly irregular spaces, large glass sections and the close proximity to

Photo: Jens Lindhe

HOUSING

Photo: Carsten Arlund, CPH City & Port Development

8House's 'street' will probably appeal mainly to people of a more outgoing disposition and preferably without too many family heirlooms.

The building's figure-of-eight shape and the twisting, rising, falling street invest the building with unpredictable, varied and fascinating outdoor spaces. On the other hand, the traditional, intimate courtyard ambience has been broken, and their size and layout do not encourage residents to use them. The darker of the two courtyards is laid out as a big bonsai tableau, while the other offers informal parking space and a playground for a kindergarten on the ground floor.

So actually the 'district' is not self-sufficient, but depends on drawing on, and interacting with its surroundings. Leisure facilities are available for residents at the adjacent PLUG N PLAY park (29), and on *Kalvebod Fælled*, while visitors can drop into the 8House café and take a stroll round Copenhagen's farthest-flung building.

VM MOUNTAIN

Ørestad Boulevard 55, København S

HOUSING

CLIENT	Dansk Olie Kompagni / Høpfner
ARCHITECT	BIG / JDS
ENGINEER	Moe & Brødsgaard
TIME	Inaugurated in 2008

The suburbs and typical residential areas were obviously an inspiration for the VM Mountain, which has been christened an 'upright suburb'. This award-winning building houses both dwellings and a parking facility with 650 spaces, so the residents have direct access to their homes, while people in the neighbourhood have been spared a car park.

Viewed from the north, the VM Mountain resembles a gigantic, high-tech machine with large metal and glass surfaces, and cars driving in and out of the spectacular parking facility with its bright, powerful colours. The north side also depicts Mount Everest by way of holes perforated in the façade's aluminium sheets. The building's dwellings have been constructed as plots stacked on top of one another, as if on a mountain slope, where the roof of the resident below is the garden of the resident above. Viewed from the south, the building has a completely different personality, with roof gardens dominated by warm, natural materials: wooden terraces, verdant climbing plants and lawns.

The building was created for modern people, who want to combine all the benefits of the city with all the qualities of the suburbs. The style is highlighted by the building's position on the site. All the terraces face the old housing district of *Vestamager*, affording a view of back gardens, do-it-yourself home extensions and Danish national flags. On the other side of the VM Mountain the style is not at all suburban. It is an almost futuristic urban scene, featuring the elevated tracks of the Metro and the new, contemporary housing complexes of *Ørestad City*.

VM HOUSES

Ørestads Boulevard 57–59, København S 　　📍 E7

👤 CLIENT	Dansk Olie Kompagni / Høpfner
✎ ARCHITECT	BIG / JDS
🔧 ENGINEER	Moe & Brødsgaard
📅 TIME	Inaugurated in 2005

As the name suggests, the VM Houses, when viewed from the air, are shaped like the letters 'V' and 'M'. The buildings represent the architects' vision of how to provide maximum light and views for the majority of residents within the confines of a limited space and while working to a relatively low construction budget. The four- to twelve-storey buildings are constructed of concrete, steel and expansive glass façades. V House offers 40 different types of apartment, M House 36, and most of them are on more than one level. The apartments interlock like building blocks of all shapes and sizes and allow room for architectural surprises, which tend to make interior decoration a bit of a challenge.

Most people first notice the pointed, triangular balconies jutting out from the façades of V House like sharp spikes. These south-facing balconies were designed so as to block the least possible light from the apartments below. To keep costs down, and to provide the apartments with the most possible light and a feeling of space and air, there are no partition walls in the apartments. So all the apartments are one-roomed. Instead, it is up to the residents themselves to shape the rooms according to their own tastes and requirements. What is more, in some places the apartments have five-meter high ceilings.

Space and air were also considerations outside. So V House is raised on five-metre-high columns to let light into the northern courtyard and to create a feeling of openness. On the southern side the building creates a warm, sunny front garden for the VM residents.

43 ØRESTAD SYD RÆKKEHUSE

Richard Mortensens Vej 100–170, København S 📍 D8

👤 CLIENT	Arkitektgruppen
✎ ARCHITECT	Tegnestuen Vandkunsten
🌿 LANDSCAPE	Bang og Linnet Landskab
🔧 ENGINEER	Henry Jensen
📅 TIME	Inaugurated in 2011

The concept of the 36 townhouses in *Ørestad Syd* stems primarily from a wish to give the area a small-scale building, and provide a contrast to the giant constructions, which otherwise characterise *Ørestad*. The black façade cladding of the buildings is also a powerful contrast to their neighbour, the white 8House (40). The terraces are staggered around a south-facing stair-street, which unites the houses and leads directly to the lakes. Terraces and rooftop terraces will provide residents with excellent views of the protected common.

44 SIGNALGÅRDEN

Amager Fælledvej 135–147, København S 📍 E5

👤 CLIENT	Boligforeningen 3B
✎ ARCHITECT	ONV Arkitekter
🌿 LANDSCAPE	Schul
🔧 ENGINEER	Dominia
📅 TIME	Inaugurated in 2011

Between *Ørestad Nord* and *Urbanplanen* on *Amager*, two aluminium-clad blocks have appeared on *Trekantgrunden*. These new, low-energy dwellings are part of the *AlmenBolig+* concept. This is low-rental, family housing, where the residents themselves can contribute to the way the apartments are fitted out, and are personally responsible for upkeep and service. The buildings have been built sustainably as assembly kits of prefabricated, room-sized modules and provide family dwellings, assisted living facilities and a day-care centre.

GYLDENRISPARKEN

Amagerbrogade / Gyldenrisvej / Store Krog, København S   📍 F6

45

Photo: Kristian Seier

👤 CLIENT   Lejerbo
✏️ ARCHITECT   Vandkunsten / WITRAZ
🌿 LANDSCAPE   Algren & Bruun
🔧 ENGINEER   Wissenberg / EKJ
📅 TIME   Renovation completed in 2011

HOUSING

Gyldenrisparken is a classic public housing development, constructed in 1966. In the renovation process, the old damaged concrete was clad with insulation material and a shell of white fibre-reinforced concrete. Meanwhile, the residents have been given new balconies, low-energy windows and bays, which protrude from the façade in a random pattern and disrupt the former monotony. The grounds have been upgraded, and the boring hedges have been replaced by a new, large playground. New assisted living facilities, an after-school clubhouse and a day-care centre have also been added.

FLINTHOLM SENIOR HOMES

Elga Olgas Vej 5, Frederiksberg   📍 B3

46

Photo: Jens Lindhe

👤 CLIENT   Frederiksberg Ejendomme
✏️ ARCHITECT   Frederiksen & Knudsen Arkitekter
🔧 ENGINEER   Lemming & Eriksson
📅 TIME   Inaugurated in 2007

This five-storey, elliptical building provides 50 dwellings for elderly people. In addition to providing access to the park, the ground floor houses all the service functions, while all accommodation is located above. The motto for the building's design was 'community is paramount'. One example of this is the interior layout, in which most conventional corridors have been abandoned, making room for spacious communal areas. The elliptical shape plays an important role. It compresses the building and reduces the number of corridors.

B3

HOUSING

👤 CLIENT	AKB / KAB / Kuben Byg
✎ ARCHITECT	ONV
🔧 ENGINEER	Viggo Madsen
📅 TIME	Inaugurated in 2012

The *Grøndalsvænge* townhouse district was constructed as part of the AlmenBolig+ concept, which offers newly built dwellings of between 103 and 130 m² at a low rent, so anyone can afford them. What helps is that the residents are personally responsible for the upkeep, including snow clearance, hedge cutting and the maintenance and cleaning of the communal areas. This can only be considered a plus in terms of strengthening the social interaction and sense of community amongst the residents. This is a central point of the *AlmenBolig+* concept.

This type of townhouse is the brainchild of ONV Arkitekter. The houses are constructed of prefabricated modular elements, a method that is both sustainable and cheap. With *Grøndalsvænge* ONV have proven that 'cheap' is not necessarily the opposite of aesthetic and functional. The elements can be assembled in a variety of ways, enabling the architects to combine site-specific and functional considerations with cheap, industrialised production. In *Grøndalsvænge* the elements have been assembled to create 83 one-, two- or three-storey houses, all clad with large fibre cement boards.

The dwellings are contained in seven terraces, none of which are the same. The terraces are laid out quite closely together around four green narrow streets, and create some intimate communal spaces between the buildings. Car parking is concentrated in the access road, which leaves space around the terraces for green areas, where neighbours can be in easy contact with one another and children can play safely.

BISPEBJERG BAKKE

Bispebjerg Bakke 20, København NV

 C1

👤 CLIENT	Haandværkerforeningens Fond
✎ ARCHITECT	Bjørn Nørgaard / Boldsen & Holm
🔧 ENGINEER	Grontmij
📅 TIME	Inaugurated in 2007

Because the artist Bjørn Nørgaard was responsible for the design of *Bispebjerg Bakke*, the creative process was very different from that of an architect. Using the concept of a musical score for his inspiration, Nørgaard modelled the first versions in clay, and the resulting building hovers in a region somewhere between sculpture and architecture.

The building winds musically through the grounds opposite *Bispebjerg Hospital*, and the height gently alternates between three and eight storeys. The undulating roof represents rhythm, the gateways are pauses, the brickwork is the bass line and the highly varied windowpanes are the descant. The concept for the building came about more than 40 years ago in a discussion between Bjørn Nørgaard and the chairman of the Association of Craftsmen in Copenhagen. They wanted to create a building with a sculptural appearance, founded on excellent craftsmanship and the very best materials. The building was constructed in line with sterling craftsmanship traditions and the project's lofty ambitions are reflected in the handcrafted copper roof and the window frames, which are made from the exclusive and highly durable jatoba wood. The red and yellow bricks were selected as a reference to the classic street blocks of *Nørrebro*, where, in the olden days, the accepted practice was to use red bricks on the street side and yellow at the back, facing the courtyard. The inside of *Bispebjerg Bakke* is also unique with windows and balconies that curve outwards and inwards, open light rooms and a dogged avoidance of straight lines. A major priority was a beautiful inflow of light and an excellent indoor environment in the apartments, all of which have either a balcony or a terrace.

49 EMALJEHAVEN

Rentemestervej 5–13, København NV 📍 C2

Photo: Dorthea Beres

👤 CLIENT	Ejendomsselskabet MH
✎ ARCHITECT	Entasis / Creo Arkitekter
🔧 ENGINEER	Oluf Jørgensen
📅 TIME	Inaugurated in 2007

The *Emaljehaven* residential complex was built on the former industrial site of the *Glud & Marstrand* metal goods factory, whose products included the 'Madam Blå' enamelled coffee pot. *Emaljehaven* unites the classic block structure with a public urban park. At first sight the five-storey façade does not reveal its interior, but the tall building is open at the corners, which gives a glimpse of the surprising space that lies behind. Three gates provide access to the park, whose features include a leafy woodland grove and an outdoor café.

50 CHARLOTTEHAVEN

Strandboulevarden 76–88, København Ø 📍 E2

Photo: Lundgaard & Tranberg Architects

👤 CLIENT	Harald Simonsens Ejendomskontor
✎ ARCHITECT	Lundgaard & Tranberg Architects
🌿 LANDSCAPE	SLA
🔧 ENGINEER	Erik Petersen
📅 TIME	Inaugurated in 2008

Charlottehaven contains 178 apartments with large, glass-enclosed balconies, penthouse apartments and roof terraces. It is built according to the block structure so typical of Copenhagen, while the façades of bluish-black, charcoal-fired brick interplay sensitively with the familiar shades of the surrounding *Østerbro* district. Sheltered from the traffic, the large courtyard houses a service centre with a gym, a swimming pool and café, and remarkable gardens with patterns created by lawn grass, purple moor grass and two-metre-tall elephant grass.

NORDLYSET

Amerika Plads 24–31, København Ø   📍 E2   51

👤 CLIENT	JM Danmark
✎ ARCHITECT	C.F. Møller
🔧 ENGINEER	Rambøll
📅 TIME	Inaugurated in 2006

Nordlyset ('The Northern Lights') was the first housing block to be completed in the new district on *Amerika Plads* (120). In the midst of old warehouses and new developments, Nordlyset stands out with its clear-cut, gleaming white façade.

The artist Ruth Campau created the coloured glass partitions, which separate the exterior balconies, investing the building with a refreshing interplay of colours. In addition to the exterior balcony, each apartment also has an interior balcony, which faces the inner courtyard.

FYRTÅRNET

Pakhusvej 2–12, København Ø   📍 E2   52

👤 CLIENT	Amerika Plads ApS
✎ ARCHITECT	Lundgaard & Tranberg Architects
🔧 ENGINEER	Midtconsult
📅 TIME	Inaugurated in 2007

Fyrtårnet marks the entrance to the new residential area on Amerika Plads. The building's 48 metres and 15 storeys make it noticeable from both the city and the water. This tower construction gets narrower and narrower as it rises, giving it a characteristic asymmetrical appearance. The building is clad in dark-grey natural slate, which gives a varied interplay of colours and harmonises with the slate roofs of the other buildings in the neighbourhood. Its integration with an older, neighbouring building, thus forming a block, was another way of perpetuating an old Copenhagen tradition in this modern district.

ØBRO 105

Østerbrogade 105–107, København Ø

E1

HOUSING

👤 CLIENT	Nordea Ejendomme
✎ ARCHITECT	C. F. Møller
🔧 ENGINEER	COWI
📅 TIME	Inaugurated in 2007

For years the site was the location of a car dealership, but now the cars have driven away, making room for a modern housing block. *Øbro 105* is surrounded by distinctive buildings from previous centuries, all of which are rich in history, detail and sculptural form, Using the details of the surrounding buildings as their starting point, the architects created a modern re-interpretation of the classic block building. So you quickly rediscover characteristic features such as bay windows, but in a modern copper-clad version with oblique angles and full-height windows. They allow the residents an excellent view up and down the street and draw light deep into the apartments. The red brickwork also pays tribute to the classic surroundings, but rounded corners lend a contemporary touch, while the glass-clad ground floor invests the heavy brickwork with a surprising lightness

Øbro 105 relates to, and initiates a dialogue with its surroundings. So successful is the result, that in 2007 the building was short-listed for the prestigious Mies van der Rohe award as "a sublime reinterpretation, which respects its surroundings without mimicking them." Inside, *Øbro 105* also came up with a number of interesting and untraditional solutions. The apartments have oblique walls and rounded corners, which create a feeling of movement and inspire creative decorative choices. All 52 apartments have either a balcony or a terrace facing the back courtyard, and placed to get the best light. If that was not enough, all the residents have the use of three large terraces on the top storey, which provide a stunning view.

STOKHUSGADE 4B

Stokhusgade 4B, København K   E3   54

👤 CLIENT	Claus Sivager / Nils Holscher
✏️ ARCHITECT	Holscher Arkitekter
🔧 ENGINEER	EKJ
📅 TIME	Inaugurated in 2007

This narrow glasshouse in *Stokhusgade* is totally exotic, its simplicity exists in glowing contrast to the historic buildings that surround it. On this tiny plot the architects managed to create room for seven storeys, united by an elegant, fascia in tombak, the mottled appearance and patina of which reflect the level of detail in the brick façades of the neighbouring buildings. The tombak strip winds up around the large glass windowpanes, which light up at night and reveal the interiors. The ground floor and basement of the building house business premises, while the remaining floors are given to apartments.

TORPEDOHALLEN

Galionsvej 1–11, Frederiksholm, København K   F4   55

👤 CLIENT	NCC Property Development / 2L
✏️ ARCHITECT	Tegnestuen Vandkunsten
🔧 ENGINEER	NIRAS
📅 TIME	Inaugurated in 2003

Torpedohallen is a fine example of 1950s engineering, a building with a clear form and simple construction. It used to be a shipyard for the construction of motor torpedo boats, but was converted into 67 luxury apartments, inspired by the 'loft apartments' of New York. The new apartments are built around the original, visible concrete columns and beams, which determine the hall's profile. Access to the apartments is via common ramps and steps, which run along both sides of the hall's internal basin, where the torpedo boats would once have been lowered into the water.

56 KRØYERS PLADS

Strandgade 85–87, København K

E4

Renderings: Vilhelm Lauritzen / COBE

HOUSING

👤 CLIENT	NCC Property Development
✎ ARCHITECT	Vilhelm Lauritzen / COBE
🌿 LANDSCAPE	GHB Landskabsarkitekter
🔧 ENGINEER	COWI
📅 TIME	To be inaugurated in 2014

First came *Luftkastellet*, the popular beach bar, where you could relax with your toes buried in sand imported from *Råbjerg Mile*. Then the Dutch star architect Erick van Egeraat came along with his controversial towers. These encountered heated opposition from local residents. Then, yet another proposal from the Danish trio of BIG, Henning Larsen and Kim Utzon, was turned down by Copenhagen City Council. Now, at long last, construction of the third and final proposal for *Krøyers Plads* has begun.

The building is clearly inspired by the surrounding historic warehouses of *Christianshavn*. As in those older buildings, the end walls of the two new buildings closest to the water face the edge of the quay, while their height is adjusted to their surroundings by 'pressing down' the corners. The design of the sloping roof surfaces and façades are also contemporary interpretations of the classic warehouse. Unlike the other two, the front of the third building will face the harbour basin with an open glass façade, which will provide a view over the harbour fairway. The building has a green façade and a green roof, and its strong focus on sustainable solutions has already won the apartments the Nordic Eco Label ('The Swan').

The public space planned around the new buildings has been designed with a focus on generating urban life and activity. On the basis of wishes and input expressed at citizens' meetings, plans include an observation terrace, a wooden jetty for walks along the quay, and steps leading down to the water, where people can sit or launch little boats.

HAVNEHOLMEN RESIDENCES

Havneholmen 48–86, København V 📍 D5

Photo: Adam Mørk

👤 CLIENT	Sjælsø Gruppen
✒ ARCHITECT	Lundgaard & Tranberg Architects
🌾 LANDSCAPE	Schønherr
🔧 ENGINEER	NIRAS
📅 TIME	Inaugurated in 2008

Like a white village, two U-shaped housing blocks stand at the water's edge, exuding a laid-back Mediterranean aura. These tall, white-rendered blocks of 5–8 storeys open up towards the harbour basin and, like the other buildings on *Havneholmen*, the mono-pitched roofs rise at an angle towards the water. In each courtyard opening a tower block juts out into the harbour, surrounded by water on three sides.

There is great variety, in terms of the size and layout of the apartments. The largest apartments are more than 200 m² with as many as four balconies and a wonderful view of the harbour. The blocks have large windows on all sides and projecting bays, while the balconies are staggered in a certain rhythm, which guarantees all 236 apartments generous sunlight and a view of the harbour. This design element also lends the façade a more complex character and creates an interesting interplay between light and shadow. In terms of their interior, the apartments have been decorated with white plaster and simple materials such as untreated teak.

The architects have paid great attention to details, which accentuate the relationship to water. A wooden deck winds its way between the buildings and into the courtyards, which have been planted with grasses resembling sea lyme and small trees, which create a sense of beach and coast. Two narrow canals direct the water right in between the buildings and reflect the light, creating an almost Venetian atmosphere in the courtyard. The apartments located directly on the canals also have small landing stages on the water.

SØMÆRK

Peter Holms Vej 9–27, København SV　　　📍 C6

Photos: Adam Mørk

👤 CLIENT	SAB v. KAB /
	Finansgruppen Nordic A/S
✎ ARCHITECT	Tegnestuen Vandkunsten
🔧 ENGINEER	Lemming & Eriksson
📅 TIME	Inaugurated in 2008

Sømærk consists of five residential blocks with parking in the basement and a communal building. This might sound a bit mundane, but it is far from it. *Sømærk* is partly constructed on piles out in the water. This suspended wing, creates an interaction between water and land, giving the building its special character.

The building was consciously designed to give the residents a powerful sense of water and harbour. The buildings are not built at the water's edge, but actually on the water. That means that many of the apartments experience a glimmering reflection of the water surface on their ceilings. There are access balconies to get from A to B, and moving about, two storeys above the water, gives the impression of walking alongside the rail of a ship.

Between the blocks there are basins, where children and other water-lovers can go swimming, when the weather permits. Under the piles, which keep Sømærk above the water, there are tables, where residents can clean the fish they have just caught in the harbour. The proximity to the harbour also means that the water level is very variable, and the wooden deck that skirts the residential blocks gets immersed from time to time.

Half of the dwellings are privately owned, and half are rented. The first block on the waterfront contains privately owned units. The next block consists of rented dwellings, and the two types of unit alternate block by block for the five blocks. The idea behind mixing different types of housing was to create an environment characterised by diversity.

METROPOLIS

Oscar Pettifords Vej 23–29, København SV   📍 D6

HOUSING

👤 CLIENT	Ejendomsselskabet Metropolis / Nordkranen	
✎ ARCHITECT	Future Systems / Danielsen Architecture	
🔧 ENGINEER	Moe & Brødsgaard	
📅 TIME	Inaugurated in 2008	

"Futuristic fantasy!" That was the sales slogan for *Metropolis*, a 40-metre tall residential building. Its round shapes, radiant light-blue colour and organic appearance would seem to support this description of the building. The building is surrounded by water on three sides, and located on the outermost peninsula of *Sluseholmen*, which was expanded by about 2,000 artificial square metres. The actual building unfolds in an elongated fan shape, which widens out the dwellings and provides a view towards the west.

A long gravelled path leads up to this weird edifice and continues all the way around the outside of the building along the edge of the water. With its basement parking this residential building has a powerful aesthetic profile, but is still somewhat enclosed within itself.

The collaboration between the Danish firm Danielsen Architecture and the English firm Future Systems resulted in a design, which draws its inspiration from classic Copenhagen architecture, but whose organic shapes and bright colours also pay lip service to international contemporary architecture. The blue colour and the texture of the façade's fibre-reinforced concrete cladding will eventually achieve a patina, which will resemble the surface of a sea shell.

The original plan gave *Metropolis* four more storeys than it finally ended up with. But such a height would have come into conflict with the smoke from the *H.C. Ørstedsværket* power station, which is located nearer to the city centre. But Metropolis has been built to allow for the addition of more storeys, should the need ever arise.

HOUSING

Photo: Adam Mørk

👤 CLIENT	Walls	
✏️ ARCHITECT	Holgaard Architects	
🔧 ENGINEER	JJ Byg	
📅 TIME	Inaugurated in 2010	

These are deluxe apartments for business people, urban cosmopolitans and well-heeled tourists. They offer a high level of service, communal facilities and a view of the harbour from the largest rooftop terrace in Scandinavia. This, in a nutshell, is the basis of the concept for the STAY Copenhagen hotel on *Islands Brygge*, which opened its doors in spring 2010. All the apartments are modelled according to a range of exclusive templates, which are not to be found in any typical apartment building. These include a spacious, one-room apartment with a shower slap in the middle of the room, and a flat with a terrace running the whole length of the façade. But there are also some more traditional apartments. The furniture company HAY have fitted out the building in a luxurious and mega modern style, completely free of all the old, Danish design clichés.

The building was originally constructed in 1963 as a workers' hotel, in connection with the legendary soyabean cake factory. It took its name from the A-shaped ground plan. Since then the building has been used as offices for the postal service and relief studios for DR. Nonetheless, for long stretches of time, *A-huset*, because of its isolated location on the edge of *Islands Brygge*, stood empty. However, starting in 2003, it was taken over by the city's creative professionals, who could rent generous space, cheaply and close to town. The building was in sad need of thorough renovation, so they had a free hand to do it up and decorate it in any way they wanted. The artist Tal R, the musician Anders Trentemøller and the designer Henrik Vibskov were just some of the many, who set up shop in *A-huset*, and in no time it became a popular night spot and cultural venue for Copenhagen.

GEMINI RESIDENCE

Islands Brygge 32, København S D5

61

Photo: Robert Hart

HOUSING

👤 CLIENT	NCC Property Development / Gemini Residence
✎ ARCHITECT	MVRDV / JJW Arkitekter
🔧 ENGINEER	Peter Lind / NCC Construction
📅 TIME	Inaugurated in 2005

The conversion of the grain silo in Copenhagen's *Havnestad* is an example of today's use of the former industrial buildings in Copenhagen's harbour. The three silos (*Frøsilo, Wennberg Silo* and *Pressesilo*) were all once part of the gigantic Soyabean Cake Factory, which spanned the full length of the waterfront on *Islands Brygge*, and was the biggest place of employment in the city. The *Frøsilo* was built in 1963 for the storage of seeds and grain, which were loaded and unloaded on a daily basis by large coasters. Now all three silos have been converted to exclusive dwellings. Frøsiloen offers 42 deluxe apartments, ranging in size from 70 m² to 180 m².

The original *Frøsilo* consisted of two raw, bare concrete cylinders, each measuring 25 metres in diameter. The challenge was how to retain the authenticity of the silo, while at the same time modernising it. Cutting openings in the concrete was difficult, and if the apartments had been located inside the silo cores, they would have faced inward, away from the surroundings and the view. So they were positioned in ring-shaped additions on to the concrete cylinders, the shape of which is still visible at street level. The outer walls of the apartments are made of glass, and their wide balconies provide optimal views of the harbour. The interior space of the two enormous, empty towers is used for the lobby, stairs, elevators and galleries. Approximately 40 metres above, at the top of each building, is a new type of climate screen made of transparent film, from which the light streams down through the galleries of the eight storeys.

77

62 BOLIGSLANGEN

Tom Kristensens Vej 6–16, København S   📍 E5

👤 **CLIENT**   FSB Bolig / Kuben Byg
✎ **ARCHITECT**   Fælledhaven: Domus Arkitekter
                 Universitetshaven: Arkitema
🔧 **ENGINEER**   Lemming & Eriksson
📅 **TIME**   Inaugurated in 2006

Boligslangen is one of the biggest housing projects in *Ørestad* with 320 dwellings and an integrated day-care centre. It owes its name to its sinuous form and the roof, which floats above the openings between the buildings. What is particularly special about Boligslangen is that one, single, continuous roof covers two separate buildings. *Fælledhaven* consists of flexible, municipal housing, while *Universitetshaven* offers privately owned apartments and co-ops. The scheme represents an attempt to create a diverse mix of residents and a positive urban environment.

63 BIKUBEN KOLLEGIET

Amager Fælledvej 50, København S   📍 E5

👤 **CLIENT**   Kollegiefonden Bikuben
✎ **ARCHITECT**   AART
🔧 **ENGINEER**   Rambøll
📅 **TIME**   Inaugurated in 2006

Because of its noticeable location at the gateway to *Ørestad Nord*, *Bikubenkollegiet* has been given a distinctively patterned façade and an orange signature colour to make it stand out. The building is designed as a spiral, in which the dormitory rooms twist past the communal areas and up through the building. As soon as you open the door of your room, you find yourself in the middle of a communal kitchen or in some other social meeting space. You can also see in both directions between all the communal areas through the inner courtyard.

HOUSING

Rued Langgaards Vej 10–18, København S E5

HOUSING

CLIENT	Nordea Danmark Fonden / Fonden Tietgenkollegiet
ARCHITECT	Lundgaard & Tranberg Architects
LANDSCAPE	Marianne Levinsen / Henrik Jørgensen
ENGINEER	COWI
TIME	Inaugurated in 2006

This round, award-winning building accommodates 400 students and encourages a high degree of communal living. One source of inspiration for the architects of this building was the traditional Tulou buildings in southeast China. These are village communities with individual dwellings and communal facilities, united in circular structures. In *Tietgenkollegiet* residents can peer over the round space in the centre and see what other people are up to in the communal areas. If something grabs their interest, they can get to it directly, because none of the passages have dead ends and none of the doors are locked, so you can walk all the way round.

The building is divided into five sections, between which are the passageways that give access from outside to the central courtyard. The ground floor has a café, function hall, study and computer room, laundry, music and conference facilities and a bicycle park. The upper storeys have residential groups of 12 rooms for each of the building's blocks. The rooms are at the top, so everyone has a view.

The central communal areas, kitchens and communal rooms are suspended almost unnaturally in the air above the inner courtyard. With a depth of up to 8 metres, these boxes posed a real challenge for the engineers, who had to seek inspiration from areas such as bridge building out at sea. On the outside of the building the façade is covered with tombak (a copper-based alloy) and oak. The inner spaces are characterised by rough concrete, while the walls are clad with birch wood veneer.

PUBLIC
BUILDINGS

76

77

ANNE SKOVBRO

Director of Development and Planning, Københavns Kommune

"WE WENT FROM URBAN RENEWAL TO URBAN DE-VELOPMENT"

Photo: Jasper Carlberg

In the city's many new public institutions, there are many indications that the city is cultivating sustainability and innovation as never before. But the needs of the city will continue to change, so "this must be incorporated into the architecture, which is being designed now," says Anne Skovbro, Director of Development and Planning at City of Copenhagen.

How would you explain the construction of so many public buildings in Copenhagen?

"Copenhagen has been in a fortunate position. The city has been in a state of growth, and there are more of us. That has certainly necessitated the creation of new institutions: particularly daycare centres and schools. We have also renovated assisted living facilities, and many institutions of higher education have been given new facilities. Copenhagen is in a completely different situation from that of just 20 years ago. Put simply, one can say that Copenhagen has changed from being an 'urban renewal city' to an 'urban development city.'"

Can one detect any particular trends in the way institutions are being built right now?

"We have ambitious goals, both to build at a higher rate, because of the many children coming to the city, but also to build sustainably. Copenhagen's goal of being CO_2-neutral by 2025 has been crucial. This makes demands on building. We have come very far on that front, but technology is constantly developing new solutions, so we will continue to look at things in new ways. Several buildings are already connected to the district cooling system, which Copenhagen is in the process of developing. It will eventually spread throughout the city in the same way as our district heating system. It is going to generate enormous energy gains.

Of course, in many places architecture reflects the current trends in areas such as learning and teaching. But the most important trend today is basically about the art of the possible. We are building within the city, so it is more the exception than the rule that there is optimal space for a new building. The school in Sydhavnen is one of those exceptions. In most cases, architectural solutions are conceived as a result of the physical limitations,

which are an inevitable condition for the construction of public institutions today."

What do you think we will see more of in the future?

"Flexible architecture, to an even greater extent than we see it today. Buildings must be converted to new purposes, in case the composition of the city changes again one day. This factor should be incorporated into the architecture being designed now. In this respect we still have a lot to learn. Among architects, there is a strong tradition of submitting proposals, which appear to be final and flawless, but we are going to need solutions, which can be much more adaptable.

Moreover, we are going to see some more of what we today call 'intelligent square metres'. In practice, we break up some of the divisions, which have tradition-ally been part of institutional buildings: for example, in which a school got one building, and a cultural centre got another. A property can certainly be used for some-thing more than its primary function. One example is the school in Ørestad, which also contains a public municipal library. While comprising one of the school's facilities, the library is also aimed outwards and is used by residents in the area. In this way square metres are better used, while, in terms of the community, these kind of solutions can generate life."

What would you recommend people to go and see?

"I think the new school in Ørestad (66) is well worth a visit. Anyone can go into the library from the street and see what the integration of the two institutions has add-ed to the local area. I would also recommend a trip to the Green Lighthouse (77) on University of Copenhagen's *Nørre Campus* (134). It is not a particularly large building, but it shows very clearly what one can achieve by think-ing in terms of form. It is the building's round shape, which underpins a large part of its energy solutions, which have attracted so much publicity for this little building. This is something really worth seeing."

65 ØRESTAD GYMNASIUM

Ørestads Boulevard 75, København S

👤 CLIENT	City of Copenhagen
✎ ARCHITECT	3XN
🔧 ENGINEER	COWI
📅 TIME	Inaugurated in 2007

The fluid borders of the space in Ørestad High School signal a resounding farewell to the strict control and clear hierarchy of the old gloomy school concept. Architecturally speaking, it is the first high school in Denmark to embrace the visions for content, subject knowledge, organisation and teaching systems, which are contained in Denmark's 2005 high school reform. Flexibility and openness are the key words for this new high school building, which has been designed in the firm belief that architecture has a powerful influence on our behaviour, and that open rooms provide a better and more flexible educational environment.

Many students arrive in Ørestad by metro and are immediately confronted with the high school's façade with its coloured shutters, which resemble the spines of books on a giant shelf, a symbol for the building's literal store of knowledge. As you enter the building, you soon become aware that something unusual is afoot. Traditional classrooms hardly exist at all in this building, while the staff room and the principal's office have been abolished like a relic from an obsolete conception of how a high school should function. Instead the building is laid out as one vast space around the central staircase, which forms the building's spine.

First comes the open foyer, which also functions as a canteen. Here the pupils can enjoy the spectacle of their gymnastic classmates in full swing, because the foyer is directly adjacent to the gymnasium, separated only by transparent, sliding panels. The wide spiral staircase winds its way up through the building and provides access to the upper storeys. At the top the spiral staircase opens out onto a rooftop terrace, which affords views over vast areas of Ørestad and Vestamager.

Photos: Adam Mørk

Nearly all movement in the building is dependent on the central staircase, which is visible from all areas, and which the architects christened 'the catwalk'. Here you can see everyone, and everyone can be seen. The building's boomerang-shaped, deck-like floors rotate around the staircase, and open areas, glass-covered compartments and simple lecture rooms create a setting for the day-to-day teaching. But out towards the building's façade you do also discover some more solitary nooks and crannies, which provide room for contemplation and concentration.

The core concepts of Ørestad High School's profile are media, communication and culture, and the high school recently introduced paperless teaching, working instead with iPads and e-books. Since its inauguration this high school building has become a mecca for architects and educational professionals from abroad, all on the lookout for inspiration for the teaching environments of the future.

Arne Jacobsens Allé 3, København S   E7

Photos: Peter Sørensen, CPH City & Port Development

CLIENT	City of Copenhagen
ARCHITECT	KHR Arkitekter /
	Bisgaard Landskabsarkitekter
ENGINEER	WSP / Cenergia
TIME	Inaugurated in 2012

A picturesque mountain village with hanging gardens, bay windows and small piazzas. The inspiration for Ørestad School and Library was the Tuscan medieval village of Barga. The result is an untraditional and attractive school building with an abundance of nooks and crannies, alleyways and partially covered terraces.

The small size of the plot was a serious impediment to the project, so an innovative concept was essential. So the architects distributed the outdoor areas of the school on a number of small terraces, distributed over the 8 storeys of the building. This creates a wealth of varied spaces and connections in the complex building, aimed at accommodating the profile of this school, whose focus is on creative subjects and innovative methods of teaching. Sustainability is a vital element, both in the school's approach to education and in the architecture. The building complies with Danish Low Energy Class 1 standard and is CO_2 neutral, while the school has its own herb garden, waste separation, a small windmill and solar panels on the roof.

The village life is not only for the school's pupils. Visitors can also climb the school via an outdoor 'step-promenade' and take part in the fun and games in the public playground. Ørestad's public library is located on the ground floor of the building and is linked internally to the school. It is available to the pupils of the school, local residents and to the neighbouring Ørestad Gymnasium (65).

Later Ørestad School will be integrated with a future school in Ørestad South, whose profile will focus on sport, health and movement. As the pupils get older, they can commute by metro between the two schools' various academic and social provisions.

IT UNIVERSITY

Rued Langgaards Vej 7, København S   📍 E5

Photo: Adam Mørk

👤 CLIENT	Statens Forsknings- og Uddannelsesbygninger
📝 ARCHITECT	Henning Larsen Architects
🔧 ENGINEER	Grontmij
📅 TIME	Inaugurated in 2004

If you walk along the canal in the direction of ITU, you are confronted by a streamlined façade of glass and steel, which can come across as somewhat cold. But once inside, you can better understand why the building has attracted so much attention. Between the two main buildings there is an impressive inner courtyard, from which all of the building's five storeys are visible. A series of conference rooms are suspended over the courtyard like 'drawers', which expose the students at work from all sides, investing the building with a buzzing sensation of life and activity.

VALBY SCHOOL

Ved Ovnhallen 6 / Porcelænstorvet 4, Valby   📍 B5

Photo: Lina Ahnhoff

PUBLIC BUILDINGS

👤 CLIENT	City of Copenhagen
📝 ARCHITECT	RIA
🔧 ENGINEER	RIA
📅 TIME	Inaugurated in 2005

Valby School and Cultural Centre has been moved into the old *Norden* Porcelain Factory. The school is situated in *Ovnhallen*, and externally the industrial features of the old factory building have been preserved. Inside, the bores from the old chimneys have been used, so the centre of the large building is completely open from floor to ceiling. The use of sliding wall panels in the building means that room divisions are flexible, and furniture and equipment can be moved around. The adjacent *Prøvehallen* has been converted to a cultural and sports centre, with halls of various sizes and a flexible layout.

69 SYDHAVN SCHOOL

Støberigade 1, København SV

Photo: JJW Arkitekter

👤 CLIENT	City of Copenhagen
✎ ARCHITECT	JJW Arkitekter
🔧 ENGINEER	NIRAS
📅 TIME	To be inaugurated 2014

Sydhavn School is the long-awaited flagship school which will attract more families with children to the new residential districts on *Sluseholmen* (130) and *Teglholmen* (129). The school, which will literally sink its teeth right into the harbour basin, will have a scientific profile, with a particular focus oceanography. A vertical façade, the full height of the building, will face the street, while on the seaward side the school will be more like a landscape that integrates with the harbour basin, with a vast wooden terrace construction. In 2012 building works were seriously delayed, when the school, which was almost completed, suffered a fire.

---

70 TAGENSBO SCHOOL

Magistervej 4, København NV

📍 C1

Photo: Thomas Mølvig

👤 CLIENT	City of Copenhagen
✎ ARCHITECT	Kjær & Richter
🔧 ENGINEER	Bascon
📅 TIME	Inaugurated in 2012

In 2008 the City of Copenhagen decided to merge the two most socially disadvantaged schools in *Nordvestkvarteret*, *Grundtvig School* and *Bispebjerg School*. The result of the merger is a school with a completely new profile, where the focus is on nutrition and outdoor activity. One day a week, lessons take place outside the classrooms. The most remarkable feature of the new school is its new multi-purpose hall, which, like a green hill, rises up out of the grassy area behind the school and can be used for running, playing and tobogganing.

Photo: Kontraframe

👤 CLIENT	OPP Pihl Arkivet
🖊 ARCHITECT	PLH Arkitekter
🌿 LANDSCAPE	Schønherr
🔧 CONTRACT	E. Pihl & Søn
📅 TIME	Inaugurated in 2009

The new *Rigsarkiv* ('National Archives') can hold enormous quantities of paper: everything from censuses and written protocols to vehicle registration records. *Rigsarkivet* consists of two rectangular, monolithic blocks, totally without windows. The 12-metre high bookcases, which provide 370 kilometres of shelving, are home to several tons of important historical documents, all carefully stored at *Kalvebod Brygge*.

The design of the building has a simple geometry with large expanses of wall. They are decorated with continuous reliefs, creating a graphic interplay of light and shadow on the façade. The reliefs are shaped like runes, a direct reference to *Rigsarkivet's* collection of documents. The pattern constantly changes, never repeating itself, over the whole surface of the wall, and there are no right angles.

On the roof of one of the archive buildings, 8 metres above ground level, there is a green promenade. It is part of the plans for a much longer green stretch, which constitutes a central idea in the overall district plan for the area (128). The relief structure of the building's façade is repeated here in the form of intersecting pathways, here and there framing a number of small seating areas with benches and sloping garden beds. Rainwater is harvested from the roof garden and then stored in a reservoir for later use. In addition, the garden is acoustically and thermally insulated and releases a humidity, which effectively regulates the temperature in the building, thus providing a sound micro climate. If you happen to cross the roof on a summer's day, you can enjoy strawberries from the raised beds in the garden.

72 N. ZAHLES GYMNASIESKOLE

Nørre Voldgade 5–7, København K

 D3

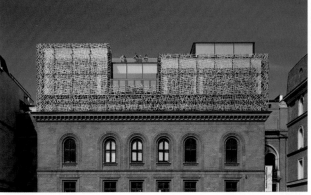

👤 CLIENT	N. Zahles Gymnasieskole
✎ ARCHITECT	Rørbæk og Møller Arkitekter
🔧 ENGINEER	Morten Sørensen
📅 TIME	Inaugurated in 2012

The preservation-worthy main building of *N. Zahles Gymnasieskole* has been modernised and raised. Two completely new storeys in glass and minimalistic filigree have sprouted up over the old school building, which was in need of more space and up to date facilities. The pupils have been given new classrooms, a new canteen and a large rooftop terrace. The bristly filigree is an architectural tribute to the branches of the large trees in *Ørstedsparken* and, when the sun hits the façade, it sketches a luxurious shadow pattern on the bright green floor of the annexe.

73 SØLVGADE SCHOOL

Sølvgade 16, København K

 E3

👤 CLIENT	City of Copenhagen
✎ ARCHITECT	C.F. Møller
🔧 ENGINEER	Esbensen / Sloth Møller
📅 TIME	Inaugurated in 2012

Sølvgade School, the oldest working school in Denmark, dating from 1847, has been expanded with 2,000 much-needed square metres. The idea was to speak the same colourful, musical language as the children, at the same time conforming to the historical, classical Copenhagen setting. So the form and colour of the school are inspired by its surroundings, for example the yellow shades of nearby *Nyboder*, which are echoed on the school's façade. The colours continue inside on the walls, the floors and the furnishings.

Blegdamsvej 9, København N   📍 D2

74

Renderings: 3XN

PUBLIC BUILDINGS

👤 CLIENT	Copenhagen University Hospital
✎ ARCHITECT	3XN
🔧 ENGINEER	Grontmij
📅 TIME	To be inaugurated in 2017

The corner of *Blegdamsvej* and *Frederik V's Vej*, opening right out to *Fælledparken*, will be the site for *Rigshospitalet's* ('Copenhagen University Hospital's') new annexe. It will be a zigzag-shaped building, which will break with the familiar square-shaped hospital structure, while its ground plan will help solve two of the hospital's major problem issues: peace near the wards and effective logistics.

Rigshospitalet's North Wing will be constructed as a series of Vs, linked by a transversal thoroughfare, effectively connecting the building's various components, providing shorter distances and making it easier and simpler for people to find their way around. Outpatient departments and other functions, which create a lot of traffic, will be kept close together on the thoroughfare. The wards will be located as far away as possible from this busy 'main street', allowing staff to move quickly from A to B without crossing through the ward sections. This will save an enormous amount of time and create a peaceful atmosphere in the vicinity of the wards.

The V structure will also create more façade space and a wonderful view of the adjacent public park, with a strong inflow of natural light into the wards. The design places a strong emphasis on pleasant and attractive surroundings, based on the theory that they have a healing effect on the patient.

The annexe will add approx. 68,000 m² to the existing *Rigshospital*, creating room for 300 single-bed wards, a surgical department, an intensive care department, outpatient facilities and an imaging department. The project will also include the construction of a 7,400 m² patient hotel and a 17,000 m² car parking facility.

THE MÆRSK BUILDING

Blegdamsvej 3B, København N

📍 D3

Rendering C.F. Møller

👤 CLIENT	Universitets- og Bygningsstyrelsen
✎ ARCHITECT	C.F. Møller
🔧 ENGINEER	Rambøll
📅 TIME	To be inaugurated in 2015

There are many witty stories about how cleverly the architects, who designed the Panum Institute, managed to conceal the entrance. There is certainly no denying, that it is quite an effort to discover the main entrance, which is tucked away in the courtyard facing *Nørre Allé*. The Mærsk Building will give the Panum Institute a new annexe, which, in addition to providing 35,000 new square metres for research and teaching, will also help to soften Panum's colossal, shut-in appearance, especially with the help of a new, more easily accessible main entrance. The new main entrance will face *Blegdamsvej*, where a forecourt will integrate the building into the street scene, thus drawing life in its direction.

Viewed from the air, the Mærsk Building looks like an irregular star, emanating from the existing Panum. Four low buildings jut out at ground level, at the same time providing the basis for a 15-storey high-rise unit. The selection of colour and materials will match the existing Panum and create a visual coherence and transition. But there the similarities end. An extensive use of glass in the façade will create a transparent appearance, so at street level the building and its surroundings will seem to coalesce.

The project also includes a new, recreational public space, which will envelop the Mærsk Building and continue the whole way to *Skt. Johannes Kirke*. Between the buildings there will be new squares and inner garden spaces with alcoves and places to sit. They will serve as an extension of the teaching areas and offices, but also constitute a green contribution to the city. Between *Nørre Allé* and *Blegdamsvej* a pedestrian and cycle path will be constructed, which will cut right across the area.

CENTRE FOR CANCER & HEALTH

Nørre Allé 45, København N   D2

Photo: Adam Mørk

CLIENT	City of Copenhagen
ARCHITECT	NORD Arkitekter
ENGINEER	Wessberg
TIME	Inaugurated in 2011

The new Centre for Cancer & Health is a modern take on how architecture can have a healing effect and actively contribute to a quicker convalescence for cancer patients after a period of illness. The building does not look like a hospital, nor does it smell like one. On the contrary, everything has been done to create a building, in which the users do not feel like patients. The key lies in building on a human scale and creating a homely atmosphere.

Viewed from outside, the centre comprises a cluster of small, individual houses, the roofs and façades of which are clad with the same light aluminium panels. The houses are laid out in a circle around an inner courtyard, and the walls on this side are clad with wood, thus creating a warm and agreeable atmosphere. The courtyard serves as a modern cloister garden with a variety of themes, where the users of the building, which include cancer patients, relatives and convalescents, can meet for a cup of coffee, cultivate vegetables or simply enjoy a quiet moment in the sunshine.

Inside, beneath the zig-zagged roof, the little houses are interconnected. Here there are common rooms and more private rooms, which are used by patient groups, psychologists, groups for relatives and for other activities organised by the Danish Cancer Society. The kitchen plays a central role in the building. Here the users gather to cook together and learn about food and nutrition as vital elements in the healing process.

The Centre is the result of collaboration between staff and users, and has focused on being a pleasant place in which to stay, without stigmatising its visitors.

Tagensvej 16, København N 📍 D2

Photos: Adam Mørk

PUBLIC BUILDINGS

👤 CLIENT	University of Copenhagen
✏️ ARCHITECT	Christensen & Co. Arkitekter
🔧 ENGINEER	COWI
📅 TIME	Inaugurated in 2009

Green Lighthouse was built in the run-up to the 2009 Copenhagen Climate Change Conference as an example of a CO_2 neutral building. The building houses the Student Service Centre of the Faculty of Science and serves as a meeting point for research workers and students. Green Lighthouse uses the newest technology to reduce energy consumption. Surprisingly, though, 70 pct. of the energy saving comes from the architecture alone, which took sustainable solutions into account from the very start.

Sun is the main source of energy in Green Lighthouse. The round shape of the building allows full exploitation of the sun's rays throughout the day. Adjustable slats in the window panels move up and down automatically with the passage of the sun around the façade and help regulate the temperature. The sloping, south-facing roof is fitted with solar cells and solar heating panels, which heat the building, produce hot water and generate all the electricity for the building's needs. The varying intensity of the sun has been incorporated into the energy system. In summer, the surplus solar energy is collected in an underground store, to be used later when the sun is at its weakest.

These are just a few of the many solutions, which reduce the energy consumption to under the 30 kWh/m² per year, which are required for the CO_2-neutral classification. But this technology is complicated and, after the first few years of the building's existence, energy consumption was double what had been expected. This was due to a fault in the ventilation system, and a series of solar cells, which someone had simply forgotten to switch on. Since correcting the faults, energy consumption has fallen, and is much closer to the original estimate.

AMAGER RESSOURCE CENTRE

Kraftværksvej 31, København S   F3

CLIENT	Amagerforbrændingen
ARCHITECT	BIG
ENGINEER	Rambøll
TIME	To be inaugurated in 2017

In traditional terms, there was always a separation between industry and leisure activities, but BIG's new incineration plants on *Amager* manage ingeniously to combine the two. The 90-metre high plants will not only convert garbage into energy, they will also serve as a giant ski slope with 1.5 kilometres of green, blue and black pistes. Meanwhile, viewing platforms on top, green surroundings, cafés, climbing walls and lots more besides, will make the plant an all-year-round destination for the whole family. Another highly imaginative subtlety is the plant's chimneys, which will send the smoke out in the form of giant smoke rings.

PUBLIC BUILDINGS

STENURTEN

Rantzausgade 53, København N   C3

CLIENT	City of Copenhagen
ARCHITECT	Arkitema
ENGINEER	NIRAS
TIME	Inaugurated in 2002

Located behind *Brorsons Kirke* on *Rantzausgade* is Copenhagen's very first ecological day-care centre. *Stenurten* is the City of Copenhagen's pilot project for urban ecology and environmentally sound planning. There is moss on the roof, flax is used for insulation. But the building also introduces ecology into the everyday lives of children and adults. To avoid putting *Brorsons Kirke* in the shade, the house has been sunken in the north east, but opens up towards the south west. Behind the large glass façade is the building's climate zone, which, in unison with the large chimneys, powers the natural ventilation system.

Photo: Anders Hviid

👤 CLIENT	City of Copenhagen
✎ ARCHITECT	JJW Arkitekter
🔧 ENGINEER	Øllgaard Rådgivende Ingeniører
📅 TIME	Inaugurated in 2009

The expansion of the after-school centre *Universet* ('The Universe') was built on the site of an existing playground, which was not a popular move in a district that is not exactly abundant in recreational areas. But, instead of choosing between the playground and the after-school centre, with one, quick master-stroke, JJW managed to create more square metres for both of them.

By raising the closed volume of the after-school centre to first-floor level, they freed an area beneath the building to become a playground. Meanwhile, the roof area is laid out as a terrace. So, overall, the construction of the new building has provided more square metres than before. The façade is clad in unique corten steel plates, all of which rust in different ways. Over time they will achieve a beautiful rust-red appearance, which will compliment the surrounding brick buildings. The after-school centre balances on a smaller building, which acts as a pedestal. The lower building's transparent glass façade enhances the concept of the first floor as a floating after-school centre. The lower part houses multi-functional rooms and club premises, which are available to everyone in the neighbourhood. This double function means there is life and energy throughout the day.

The building complies with the strict Danish Low Energy Class 1 standard. Because the building is raised up amongst the treetops, there is shade in the summer, while in the winter it is exposed to the sun. At the same time, despite the centre's urban setting, the children experience a sense of nature and the cycle of the seasons. Meanwhile, the staggered placing of the windows provides plenty of daylight, but avoids overheating on hot days.

SJAKKET

Skaffervej 4–6, København NV

Photo: Kontraframe

Photo: Vegar Moen

👤 CLIENT	City of Copenhagen / Sjakket / Realdania
✎ ARCHITECT	PLOT (BIG/JDS)
🔧 ENGINEER	Birch & Krogboe
📅 TIME	Inaugurated in 2007

Sjakket ('The Gang') is a sanctuary for socially disadvantaged children and young people, some of whom are predisposed to crime, where they can receive support to get back on the straight and narrow. The young people can go to classes, meet up with friends, practice sport, play music or just hang out. Since 1995 *Sjakket* has been housed in a disused printing factory from 1938, which had gradually become so dilapidated, that it was unhealthy to be in. So in 2005 a much-needed total renovation started and, after two years, the new *Sjakket* was ready to open its doors.

The old factory building consists of two, arched halls, connected by a low, central section. The building is worthy of preservation, so there was a limit to how much the architects were permitted to change. Externally the building has retained its original form, but with the addition of a red music studio, which lies like a beam across the depression between the two halls, and a small rooftop terrace.

Inside, the building's various functions are divided between the two halls. One contains administration, a school, a common room, a kitchen and a Thai-boxing studio, while the other has been designed as a flexible, multi-purpose hall, which can be used by *Sjakket* or other institutions, and young people from *Mjølnerparken*. This part can be opened, so the town and building can come into contact with one another.

Large, bubble-shaped skylights provide an excellent inflow of light into the common room and classroom, while the gable windows in the multi-purpose hall have been replaced with coloured, laminated glass.

82 FREDERIKSBERG GYMNASIUM

Falkoner Plads 2, Frederiksberg C4

Photo: Kontraframe

CLIENT	City of Frederiksberg /
ARCHITECT	Henning Larsen Architects
ENGINEER	Moe & Brødsgaard
TIME	Inaugurated in 2004

This high school is part of the total plan for *Frederiksberg's* squares (21). The assembly hall and canteen face the surrounding city, while open façades make activity, both inside and outside, visible. From the assembly hall the wide staircase gives access to flex rooms and a gymnasium on the lower floor. The two top floors are designed as a light and transparent study village with visual contact across corridors and inner courtyards. A fan of both open and more closed rooms provides flexibility for teaching and group work. Small green gardens constitute 'school yards' inside the building.

83 CBS KILEN

Kilevej 14, Frederiksberg B4

Photo: Jens Lindhe

CLIENT	Copenhagen Business School
ARCHITECT	Lundgaard & Tranberg Architects
LANDSCAPE	Marianne Levinsen /
	Algreen & Bruun
ENGINEER	NIRAS
TIME	Inaugurated in 2005

This wedge-shaped building with its movable wooden shutters, coloured glass and metal is all at once lively and elegant. Inside, an organically shaped atrium courtyard rises to a height of five storeys. Circular windows let light in from above, creating fascinating light and shadow effects in the courtyard. The rooms are located on the outer edge of the building, while the corridors wind round like indoor balconies, and a spiral staircase unites the building's storeys. *Kilen* rests on two grassy hillocks, creating an elegant finish to *Frederiksberg's* squares (21).

Howitzvej 32, Frederiksberg · C4

👤 CLIENT	Agency for Palaces & Cultural Properties	
✎ ARCHITECT	3XN	
🌿 LANDSCAPE	Schønherr	
🔧 ENGINEER	Lemming & Eriksson	
📅 TIME	Inaugurated in 2012	

Hack Kampmann's old, neo-classical, listed courthouse from 1921 has been extended with a completely new annexe, containing new courtrooms and offices. The ambition was to create a building, which, in purely architectural terms, would create a sense of gravity, but also make people feel welcome. Security and witness protection were also vital elements for the architects to deal with. Therefore, the layout of the building ensures that witnesses, defendants, judges and families of the involved parties do not meet accidentally before they enter the courtroom. For the same reason, all windows in the courtrooms are placed above eye level to guard the rooms from prying eyes.

Because the plot is comparatively small, and because it was necessary to retain an area of open space around the existing, listed courthouse, the layout of the new courthouse is extremely compact. The building is at once classical and modern. The curved shape of the roof is a contemporary interpretation of the traditional saddle roof, while the light-coloured brick façade relates to the style of the surrounding buildings, but also invests the building with its own contemporary identity.

All users of the building, with the exception of the defendants, have access to an oblong atrium, which divides the five-storey structure into two halves and serves as a source of natural light for all floors. The use of natural light is one of several energy-saving elements, which also include natural ventilation, solar shading, thermo active floors and solar power cells.

TRADE & INDUSTRY

Photo Kontraframe

THOMAS BOISEN

Managing Director, Nykredit Properties

"WE MUST PROMOTE A GREAT BUILDING CULTURE"

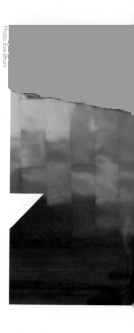

Photo: Éva Órum

The finance company, Nykredit is one of the developers responsible for Krystallen and the large public plaza, which surrounds it. The company has donated a plot of land to Kalvebod Bølge, which will help revitalise Kalvebod Brygge on the waterfront. Additionally, Nykredit has a foundation, which every year awards Scandinavia's largest architectural prize. "We have a responsibility to promote and recognise good architecture," says Thomas Boisen, Managing Director of Nykredit Properties.

What does architecture mean for a private company like Nykredit?

"Basically the building is a workplace, which needs to serve both employees and customers. But the architecture turns it into something more. That is how the building gets its DNA. It assumes a meaning for the company's values and the society of which we are a part. Particularly in terms of Krsytallen it is expressed in the way the building relates to its surroundings. An extensive plaza was created around the building, specifically to underpin the interplay between our neighbours and the rest of the city. Nykredit is part of Danish society. That is what the architecture reflects. At the same time the company finances up to 40 pct. of the loans granted for construction in the country. So our goal is also to help promote a good building culture. Quality increases conservation value, so both socially and in terms of business, it is of great importance for the company."

What trends have characterised commercial building?

"Sustainability is a very prominent feature in recent commercial buildings. There are extremely high standard requirements, when constructing a new building in Copenhagen, which naturally also affects the buildings' expression. Take the glass that covers the whole of *Krystallen*. Glass is one of the most indestructible building materials available, and it makes great sense to use it today, where you can take advantage of sunlight, insulate the building and gain many other environmental benefits, which stone, for example, does not provide. Glass is also transparent. Buildings in large public settings such as the harbour should not be dense and closed-in, so that they block the view.

Many of the existing commercial buildings were built in times when the attitude to work was very differ-

ent. Today, we need buildings in which spaces can be organised more flexibly. We have completely open floors, where people can move back and forth. This enables people to see what other people are doing. You can change the day-to-day organisation without having to rebuild the whole building. The building creates a pulse, which helps make the workplace vibrant and dynamic, and at the same time allows it to adapt to reality."

What do you expect will be important for future commercial construction?

"Sustainable construction will continue to shape the main agenda for the construction industry. It also includes a building's durability, both physically and architecturally. It is, of course, because this is extremely important in terms of society, but there is also a fundamental economic factor. It is not sensible business to invest in, or in our case to lend money for buildings, which do not live up to the standards our society sets for quality and durability.

Secondly, the city's infrastructure will probably have an impact on how new commercial buildings become part of the cityscape. We see a trend pointing towards softer modes of transport, and there is every indication that proximity to the metro and commuter trains will influence where new buildings are constructed in the future. In this context Ørestad and Nordhavn can both be very attractive areas. For a company, it is of great significance that employees have reasonable facilities for getting to and from work, in a way that can fit in with the other aspects of their lives."

What would you recommend people to go and see?

"Go and see Krystallen. From Polititorvet you can clearly see the building's apex, which is raised above the open public space, with water fountains, which are a source of delight to most children on a hot summer's day. If you walk all the way around the building, you can experience just how changeable the building's expression is. Light, reflections and shapes endlessly change character. In the evening the special lighting on the plaza creates a totally unique ambience."

85 SEB BANK & PENSION

Bernstorffsgade 50, København V

👤 CLIENT	Skandinaviska Enskilda Banken AB
✎ ARCHITECT	Lundgaard & Tranberg Architects
🌾 LANDSCAPE	SLA
🔧 ENGINEER	Rambøll
📅 TIME	Inaugurated in 2010

A challenging site surrounded by monumental buildings (the Copenhagen Postal Centre, the National Archives, the railway goods terminal and one of the busiest intersections in the city) was what the architects had at their disposal, when the banking corporation SEB commissioned their new Danish headquarters. But the building turned out to be one of the finest examples of what a headquarters could be. It blends with its surroundings and gives more back to the city than the space it took away.

Consisting of two elegant towers in shades of dark green and brown, the building rises out of dramatically landscaped grounds. The landscape bears a striking resemblance to a stylised Swedish mountainside, with birch and pine trees sloping up from street level to the height of the second floor. If you follow the sharp hairpin bends of the concrete ramp upwards, you reach an elevated green promenade, which stretches past the National Archives and Tivoli Hotel, and at a later point will be extended across *Dybbølsbro*. Steps and inclined surfaces create terraces and niches, where you can sit and watch the traffic at one of the city's busiest intersections or the skaters, who have also discovered the opportunities provided by this new, multi-levelled public space.

The organic shapes of the two towers are accentuated by the materials. Glass sections in various shades of green are framed in copper, which will gradually become coated with verdigris. Glass sections create a simple rhythm, investing the façade with a harmonious pattern. But there is nothing boring about its appearance, because an underlying, 'random' pattern of dark green

Photos: Adam Mørk

boards creates variety. The heights of the storeys also vary. The second from the top and second from the bottom are higher than the others and thus create a kind of frame around the buildings.

The core of the the building's interior is a row of concrete cylinders, which are load-bearing structures, but also contain staircases, lifts, toilets and service rooms. Each floor consists of a large open-plan space with work areas positioned alongside the rows of windows on the façade. Communal facilities are located near the centre, providing an indirect view down through the central atrium, the shape of which changes as you move around, because each floor has its own individual design. As on the façades, inside the building too, great attention has been given to materials and the interplay between the rough and the more refined details. One example is the contrast between the rough concrete surfaces and a banister in soft leather, which guides people throughout the buildings.

86 KRYSTALLEN

Kalvebod Brygge 4, København V

E4

Photo: Adam Mørk

👤 CLIENT	Nykredit Ejendomme
✒️ ARCHITECT	schmidt hammer lassen architects
🌿 LANDSCAPE	SLA
🔧 ENGINEER	Grontmij
📅 TIME	Inaugurated in 2011

Compared to the square boxes that stand side by side on the waterfront of *Kalvebod Brygge*, *Krystallen* ('The Crystal') is almost floating. The building rests on only three supports, thus providing public space under and around itself.

The idea of this area was to create a thoroughfare that would connect the city and the harbour. Just as *Krystallen's* exterior alters according to the weather, the public plaza is also in a constant state of change. In the daytime 2,000 water jets divide it into smaller spaces with 'walls' created by the water shooting up, changing shape as the wind blows and people move about. At the same time a sheet of water reflects the ever-changing light and colours of the sky.

The interior of the building is flexible and easy to decorate and fit out, because of the absence of columns. In fact, the façade is the load-bearing element in the construction, and its rhomboid pattern accentuates the building's crystalline character. To enter the building you have to walk under it. The slate paving of the plaza continues through the revolving doors, enhancing the impression that the building is something light and airy, which has just landed.

All floors are designed like a giant 'Z' around two atria, which guarantee every work space a view and natural light. Energy savings and sustainable solutions are also a priority for *Krystallen*. The roof is covered by solar cells and the three-layer glass façade offers highly efficient heat insulation. Rainwater is harvested and used to flush toilets, while seawater is used for additional cooling of the building in the summer.

HM2

Mitchellsgade 2, København V   📍 E4   87

Rendering: DISSING+WEITLING

👤 CLIENT   HM2 – HAFONN
✏️ ARCHITECT   DISSING+WEITLING
🔧 ENGINEER   Søren Jensen Rådgivende
               Ingeniørfirma
📅 TIME   To be inaugurated in 2015

The HM2 office block will be built on one of the last available sites at *Kalvebod Brygge*. The site is located between the old neighbourhood around *Glyptoteket* and *Kalvebod Brygge's* new, contemporary architecture. This was what inspired the architects. Indoor atria and backyards will guarantee an excellent inflow of daylight, at the same time paying homage to the old blocks, while the use of high-tech materials and glass façades will unite HM2 with its modern surroundings. The ground floor will be open to the public with a café and shops, in the hope of contributing to a lively neighbourhood.

TOLDBODGADE 13

Toldbodgade 13, København K   📍 E4   88

Photo: BBP Arkitekter

👤 CLIENT   LAC Toldbodgade ApS
✏️ ARCHITECT   BBP Arkitekter
🔧 ENGINEER   Orbicon
📅 TIME   Inaugurated in 2012

A somewhat dull-looking office block at Toldbodgade 13 was renovated. Its new façade invests the building with a character appropriate to the surroundings. The building was extended at the front by two metres and is now flush with the other buildings. The new façade is dressed with a 'pleated curtain' of perforated, golden-coloured metal sheets, which can be pulled up and down for solar shading. From a distance the façade mimics the classic brickwork of its surroundings, but close up it reveals the neat, vivacious pattern created by the perforation.

TRADE & INDUSTRY

109

89 THE ALLER BUILDING

Havneholmen 33, København V

👤 CLIENT	Carl Aller Etablissement
✎ ARCHITECT	PLH Arkitekter
🌿 LANDSCAPE	Schønherr
🔧 ENGINEER	Søren Jensen Rådgivende Ingeniørfirma
📅 TIME	Inaugurated in 2009

"An archetypically masculine building," is how Jan Christensen, Copenhagen's former city architect, described this building. The Aller media company consolidated all their activities in a new headquarters in Copenhagen Harbour, On the outermost pier of *Havneholmen*, PLH Arkitekter created an eight-storey building in glass, steel and aluminium. The architects made an analysis of the staff's work patterns and designed the building to cater for their needs. This led to the choice of glass and transparency, facilitating contact between the staff of the various editorial departments. In December 2009 the City of Copenhagen awarded the building the title of 'best office building', in recognition of its design and interior decoration.

The pier is triangular in shape and so is the building, which stands like an icebreaker sailing through the city's harbour. From its tip you can look down along the curved façades of glass and aluminium, which allow a constant inflow of light from all three sides. The vast glass façade enables daylight to flood into the large atrium, which cuts right through the building from south to east. The palette of materials used in the atrium (granite, oak, walnut and frosted glass) is intended to reflect the varied landscapes and changing seasons of Scandinavia. A spiral-shaped light sculpture composed of white and blue lamps reaches from the bottom of the building to the very top and serves, when viewed from *Bryggebroen* bridge (110), as a symbol for the building.

The building makes full use of its special location in the harbour and pumps seawater into the building for the purpose of cooling.

BELLA SKY HOTEL

Center Boulevard 5, København S   📍 E7

Photo: Adam Mørk

👤 CLIENT	Bella Center
✎ ARCHITECT	3XN
🔧 ENGINEER	Rambøll / EKJ
📅 TIME	Inaugurated in 2011

Its 814 rooms, 32 conference suites, three restaurants, Sky Bar and wellness centre make Bella Sky the biggest hotel in Scandinavia. Probably the wonkiest as well. Bella Sky is connected to the Bella Center and consists of two towers, rising to a height of 76.5 metres. For reasons of flight safety, it was not possible to build a high tower so close to nearby Copenhagen Airport. But we are not talking about just two ordinary skyscrapers. Bella Sky's two towers tilt in opposite directions at a gradient of sixteen degrees. A decision taken by the architects to avoid the two towers blocking each other's views. The extreme tilt (double that of the leaning tower of Pisa) was an enormous challenge for the engineers.

The towers lean 20 metres out at the top in relation to the bottom. Not only that, but the top ten floors of one tower bend out at an angle of 12 degrees, making the tower virtually twist at the top. Meanwhile, the other tower bends similarly, only at the bottom. The two towers were constructed out of prefabricated concrete elements, and are the first ever, tilted, pre-cast structure in the world. The incredible efficiency of the building process meant that each storey took only 11 days to attach.

The slanting lines continue in the façade, where triangular elements in aluminium and glass create a particularly dynamic pattern, as a compliment to the twists and turns of the two towers. Inside Bella Sky has been designed as an innovative, light, Scandinavian take on the classic hotel interior, with Danish designer furniture and green walls with living plants. In addition, Bella Sky has one floor exclusively for use by women, which, despite fierce debate, still exists.

TRADE & INDUSTRY

91 | CABINN METRO HOTEL

Arne Jacobsens Allé 2, København S   E7

CLIENT	Cabinn
ARCHITECT	Niels Fennet
FAÇADE	Daniel Libeskind
ENGINEER	Moe & Brødsgaard
TIME	Inaugurated in 2009

In 1986 the world-famous architect Daniel Libeskind wrote a symphony. When the CEO of a hotel chain talked to him about this project, Libeskind thought what the area needed was music. So, instead of a traditional façade, the end wall is decorated with a pattern inspired by the architect's musical score. The actual design and operation of this gigantic building were the job of Hotel Manager Niels Fennet, who is also an engineer.

Cabinn Metro Hotel consists of two intersecting buildings: one low, straight building along *Arne Jacobsens Allé*, and a higher, curved building along *Center Boulevard*. Both parts of the building are clad with aluminium panels. To grab attention at the exit from the airport motorway, the building was given pillar-box red end walls and blue façades, dotted with windows that resemble those perforated sheets you hang tools on. Its 710 rooms and 1,760 beds make it the one of the biggest hotels in Denmark.

Niels Fennet got the idea for the hotel's concept, while on board the Oslo ferry. He noticed how the functional layout of the cabins managed to save space without compromising comfort.

If you are interested in town planning, the hotel also sports another exciting feature. To the right of the foyer you can see a seven-metre long model of the whole of *Ørestad* on a scale of 1:1000. It provides an exceptional overview of the area's individual buildings, the four separate districts and its proximity to both Copenhagen City and the *Fælled*. The hotel is open 24 hours a day, and you are always welcome to drop in for a look at the model.

Photo: CPH City & Port Development

CLIENT	SG Nord
ARCHITECT	DISSING+WEITLING
ENGINEER	Midtconsult
TIME	Inaugurated in 2009

At first sight there is nothing green about the 85-metre high, glossy black Crowne Plaza Copenhagen Towers hotel, which rears its head like an imposing city gate to Ørestad South at the intersection between the railway, the motorway and the metro. But the streamlined façade conceals a building, which sets completely new standards in terms of modern, ecological architecture.

For example, the hotel has the biggest incorporated solar cell system in northern Europe with 2,500 m² of solar panels integrated into the black glass façade. It also has Denmark's very first groundwater-based cooling and heating system, which saves up to 90 pct. of the energy consumption for cooling and heating the hotel. The choice of every fixture and fitting, including reading lamps and hair-dryers, was based on their energy consumption, while the bathrooms are stocked with biodegradable products made from corn and potato starch instead of plastic. Crowne Plaza Copenhagen Towers has won several prestigious awards, the last in October 2010 as the world's greenest hotel.

Crowne Plaza consists of a 25-storey skyscraper, with reception and guest facilities on the ground floor, a 7-storey conference centre and, in the basement, a ballroom with space for 800 guests. The underground car park is topped by a terraced park area.

As with the environment, the hotel's recruitment of staff has also adopted an alternative approach. In association with Hvidovre Municipality and the City of Copenhagen, the hotel has established a training programme, giving new Danes from all over the world direct access to the labour market.

TRADE & INDUSTRY

RAMBØLL

Hannemanns Allé 53, København S 📍 E8

Photo: Adam Mørk

👤 CLIENT	SEB	
✎ ARCHITECT	Mikkelsen Arkitekter	
👩 LANDSCAPE	Schønherr	
🔧 ENGINEER	Rambøll	
📅 TIME	Inaugurated in 2010	

This large, boomerang-shaped building is linked together by an inner street on several levels. The architects found inspiration in Barcelona's lively shopping street, *La Rambla*. Rambøll's 'Rambla' winds both horizontally and vertically, via inset mezzanines and balconies. Like a vast moving pavement, it leads both staff and visitors effortlessly round between the eight storeys.

The large communal space on the ground floor of the building brings together facilities such as a café and canteen, a gym, foyer and auditorium, providing the staff with opportunities for informal social interaction. The goal was that the architecture should underpin the company's key values of openness, knowledge-sharing and teamwork. Another priority was to create a clear transition from the social communal areas to the peaceful office areas. The staff sit in small pockets, secluded from the building's active flow and located close to the façades, so everyone has a view and natural light.

The building's Rambla is not for the exclusive use of the building's users. It is also open to the public, and the café has outdoor waiter service, so the building also makes an active contribution to the creation of a vibrant environment in Ørestad South.

The building has been equipped with a number of eco solutions, which guarantee that its energy consumption can be kept at 10 pct. below the mandatory level. Solar cells on the roof generate energy for the building, which also has a groundwater cooling system. The ventilation is demand-controlled, which adapts to the air flow and creates a better quality indoor climate. Heat from machines and electrical equipment is recycled and rainwater is harvested for flushing toilets.

FERRING

Kay Fiskers Plads 11, København S

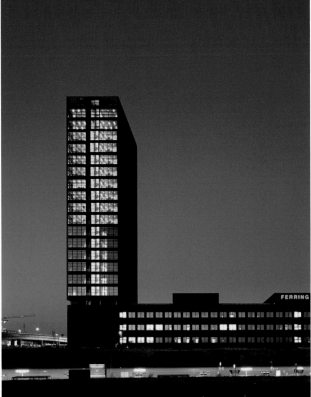

Photo: Jens Lindhe

👤 CLIENT	Nieuw Friesland
✏️ ARCHITECT	Henning Larsen Architects
🔧 ENGINEER	Moe & Brødsgaard
📅 TIME	Inaugurated in 2001

Its distinctive 20-storey, black tower and its location in a traffic nerve centre make the headquarters of the international pharmaceutical company, Ferring, one of *Ørestad* City's landmarks. It was back in 2001 that Ferring's employees moved into the new office building, making them Ørestad City's very first residents. Viewed from *Malmö*, the tower looks like a black streak in the sky, and if you stand close and look up the length of the building, you can easily get dizzy. In Copenhagen terms, a 20-storey building is still very high.

The building comprises two sections, which are designed in accordance with the functions they contain. Ferring's laboratories are located in a three-storey building, which encloses two green garden spaces. The laboratories face west, away from the crowds in the vicinity of the Metro and Field's. The company's administrative offices are located in the tall, 20-storey tower, whose façade consists of glass, with horizontal, black varnished metal slats on the outside. Viewed from outside, the slats invest the building with a certain rhythm and simple, elegant appearance. Viewed from within, they provide an excellent oblique view. The foyer is in the basement, at the same level as *Kay Fiskers Plads* outside. The transition between outside and inside is defined only by the large, glass sections, because the paving out on the square is repeated on the floor of the foyer.

In 2009 the Ferring building acquired two new, lower towers, which were also designed by Henning Larsen Architects. A new plaza was also constructed in front of the building, making a valuable contribution to life and activity in *Ørestad*.

TRADE & INDUSTRY

95 HORTEN

Philip Heymans Allé 7–9, Hellerup

Photo: Adam Mørk

CLIENT	Carlsberg Ejendomme / Horten
ARCHITECT	3XN
ENGINEER	Rambøll
TIME	Inaugurated in 2009

It could easily be mistaken for serving a purely ornamental purpose, but the façade of the Horten law firm's new office building on *Tuborg Havn* is that and much more. The architects incorporated a number of sustainable solutions, which help substantially to reduce the the building's energy consumption.

The façade is constructed of specially designed elements, which consist of two layers of fibreglass material, sandwiching a filling of high-insulating foam. It took two years to develop these fibreglass elements, which makes the Horten building something of a pioneer project. Fibreglass is used extensively in the construction of ships and windmills, but not for regular building purposes. The elements create a three-dimensional façade with north-facing windows, which create shade and reduce the need for cooling, but without taking away the view of the water. So the very architecture helps reduce the building's energy consumption, which is 10 pct. lower than the current legal requirement.

The façade is clad with light, natural travertine, which represents a re-interpretation of the classic stone-clad office building. Depending on where one stands, the three-dimensional façade changes character: at one moment a light-coloured cliff face, then a marine blue glass façade or a geometric pattern of sloping vertical and horizontal bands.

Inside, the many offices are placed around a central atrium, instead of the average corridor system, and the building's common areas are inspired by Italian piazzas, natural assembly points with space for informal meetings and inter-departmental communication.

SAXO BANK

Philip Heymans Allé 15, Hellerup

Photo: Adam Mørk

👤 CLIENT	Carlsberg Ejendomme / Saxo Bank	
✎ ARCHITECT	3XN	
🔧 ENGINEER	Rambøll	
📅 TIME	Inaugurated in 2008	

Saxo Bank is a young, in-ternet-based bank, whose main area of interest is online trading in cur-rency and stocks. If the bank stands out from the crowd, their headquarters could also be said to be some-what untraditional in banking terms. Historically speak-ing, solid buildings in heavy materials and static shapes have been banks' way of signalling credibility and solidity. But Saxo Bank decided to go in a different direction. The building was designed when the financial bubble had reached its zenith, so it seems as if this imposing head-quarters intended to encapsulate a generous measure of optimism for the future.

Together with the clients, the architects sought to strike a fine balance between dynamic expressiveness and credible solidity. The façade is alive, curving in sev-eral directions. The dynamic shape is underpinned by the façade's triangular glass sections, alternately white and transparent, which create an irregular, harlequin-like pattern.

This dynamic idiom continues inside. The six sto-reys are structured as a sequence of piled-up 'U's, and each storey is turned 180 degrees, so that no two storeys are the same. So startling spaces unfold around a large spiral staircase, which is placed in the centre of the light, open atrium. Above the staircase an enormous skylight sends natural light all the way down to the bottom of the atrium. This lower area acts as a gallery for Saxo Bank's extensive art collection, alongside a Formula One car, racing bikes and stuffed animals, all intended to inspire, challenge the senses and emphasise the progressive at-mosphere.

TRADE & INDUSTRY

97 PUNKTHUSENE

Phillip Heymans Allé 1–5, Hellerup

Photo: Tom Jersø

👤 CLIENT	Carlsberg Ejendomme
✎ ARCHITECT	Vilhelm Lauritzen Architects
🔧 ENGINEER	Rambøll
📅 TIME	Inaugurated in 2009

With their delicate green façades and rounded organic shapes, *Punkthusene* really stand out from the crowd. At first sight the three towers are the same, but subtle dislocations in the ground plan and façade give each individual building its own identity. The rhythmic waves of the façade are created by elongated window sections and touches of ornamental glass, which change expression according to the light and invest the façade with life. Inside, all the workspaces are located alongside the windows to provide maximum natural light and pleasant views. Open atria provide visual and spatial connection between the various floors.

98 HARBOUR HOUSE II

Sundkrogsgade 17–19, København Ø   📍 E1

Photo: Lars Jørgensen

👤 CLIENT	Clipper Group / Unionkul Holding
✎ ARCHITECT	Kim Utzon Arkitekter
🔧 ENGINEER	Wessberg
📅 TIME	Inaugurated in 2010

In the so-called 'Utzon Corner' of *Kalkbrænderihavnen*, Harbour House II is the latest addition to a complex of buildings designed as a unified whole by the Utzon family. The new office block, like Harbour House (2005) and the *Paustian* furniture store, is designed in a rigorous idiom. Clear, straight lines and large roof surfaces, supported by white, tree-like concrete columns, are the main features of this light building, which also contains an extension at the back of the *Paustian* furniture store. The two buildings are linked by a wide staircase, a plinth and a triangular plaza.

TRADE & INDUSTRY

Marmorvej 51, København Ø   E2

Photos: Peter Sørensen, CPH City & Port Development

👤 CLIENT	CPH City & Port Development
✎ ARCHITECT	3XN
🔧 ENGINEER	Orbicon / E. Pihl & Søn
📅 TIME	To be inaugurated in 2013–2014

Like a shining white star, UN City sits on the tip of *Marmormolen* in the old free port. It is at once enticing and unapproachable. For security reasons, UN City is built on its own artificially constructed island, which is not publicly accessible. Luckily 3XN have been able to honour both security and beauty, creating a unified, spectacular whole.

Its 45,000 m² make this UN City the sixth largest in the world. It will be home to the seven UN organisations based in Denmark. While supporting a sound and efficient working relationship between the organisations, the architecture must express the UN's values and authority. Efficiency and professionalism are balanced by dynamism and openness in this star-shaped building, which opens up to embrace its surroundings. The eight 'fingers' radiate from a central atrium, which reaches up through the whole building and connects the foyer level with all the office levels.

As well as security, sustainability has also been a high priority. Energy-saving solutions will lower UN City's energy consumption to less than 50 kWh per m² per year, which is lower than that of an average household. For example, the roof is covered in a 5,000 m² solar cell facility, which will provide green energy for lighting and heat, while green areas will harvest rainwater, which can then be recycled in the toilets.

In honour of its sustainable profile, in 2012 UN City received the prestigious Green Building Award, which is awarded by the European Commission.

TRADE & INDUSTRY

100 ANKERET

Amerika Plads 38, København Ø

📍 E2

👤 CLIENT	City Development
✏️ ARCHITECT	C. F. Møller
🔧 ENGINEER	Orbicon
📅 TIME	Inaugurated in 2008

Schizophrenically, this residential and office building has two nicknames. The north section is the headquarters of the Camilo Eitzen shipping line, so is known as Camilo Eitzen House. Meanwhile, the south section is known as *Ankeret* because, while excavating for the basement, the builders hit a big, ancient anchor. Despite their totally different functions, the dwellings and the business premises appear as one, thanks to the cohesive effect of the façade. The building is intersected by two passageways, which provide access to the courtyard space, which is shared by everyone in the two buildings.

101 ATP OFFICE BUILDING

Langelinie Allé 47, København Ø

📍 F2

👤 CLIENT	ATP Ejendomme
✏️ ARCHITECT	Lundgaard & Tranberg Architects
🔧 ENGINEER	COWI
📅 TIME	To be inaugurated in 2014

The warehouse-like buildings out at Langelinie are lined up like a string of beads. The latest 'bead' is a modern office building with a sustainable profile. The façades are broken up by a series of dormers and windows of various sizes, which lend the building a distinctive expression. The relatively small window areas, as compared to large panorama windows, will waste less heat in cold periods, while providing solar shading, when the weather is warm. A large atrium creates connections throughout the building with transverse footbridges, mezzanines and an open staircase.

TRADE & INDUSTRY

CLEANING FACILITIES

Hauser Plads 5, København K   📍 E3

102

Photo: Ty Stange

👤 CLIENT	City of Copenhagen
✎ ARCHITECT	KBP.EU – Karres en Brands & POLYFORM
🔧 ENGINEER	Oluf Jørgensen
📅 TIME	Inaugurated in 2011

A drab underground car park beneath *Hauser Plads* (37) was closed. In its place the city was given an ultra-aesthetic, horizontal office block, whose organic whiteness and transparency are reminiscent of modern Japanese architecture. The Cleaning Facilities Centre is located modestly below ground. Here, curved glass façades look out onto an interior courtyard, which fills the building with natural light. Meanwhile, the square above has been designated as a new, hilly urban playground, where those of a childish disposition can seek refuge from the frenzied bustle of the inner city streets.

COPENHAGEN FISH MARKET

Havnegade 23–25, København K   📍 E4

103

Rendering: Geisler & Nørgaard

KØBENHAVNS FISKEMARKED

👤 CLIENT	Geisler & Nørgaard
✎ ARCHITECT	Jimmy Richter Lassen
🔧 ENGINEER	Troelsgaard
📅 TIME	To be inaugurated in 2014

Soon there will be a floating fish market moored in front of the newly renovated *Havnegade*. The fish market project has been in the pipeline for a long time, and in the process the design had to be changed. The original concept was a transparent, glass fleet. The final design also includes some use of orange canvas screens. The 300 m² deck will house stalls selling fresh fish and a bar serving light fish snacks and delicacies. From the waterside you will be able to 'sail in', 'park' and shop.

INDUSTRIENS HUS

Rådhuspladsen 1, København V 📍 D4

Photo: Jens Lindhe

👤 CLIENT	Dansk Industri
✎ ARCHITECT	TRANSFORM
🔧 ENGINEER	E. Pihl & Søn
📅 TIME	To be inaugurated in 2013

Soon the neon signs on *Industriens Hus* will be switched on again. The building has been given a completely new appearance as part of the pervasive trend for expansion and renovation. It was way back in 1972 that *Industriens Hus* entered the scene on the prominent corner between *Vesterbro* and the city centre. Like other major cities at that time, Copenhagen wanted a venue in which to display the many marvels that resulted from the recent industrialisation of society. The architect Vilhelm Klein designed the building for the Scandinavian Industry and Art Exhibition, and the building was regularly modified. In 1950 the first neon signs appeared on the roof of the building, defining the identity, which was perpetuated by the architect Erik Møller in 1979 in his design for *Industriens Hus*.

Now the building is about to re-emerge in a larger, more modern incarnation. Its façade resembles something between sheets of gelatine and the diamond-shaped pattern of a harlequin costume. The façade is a double-layered construction with soundproofing properties and will reflect the old buildings on *Rådhuspladsen*. In sunny weather the enormous building will seem to dissolve in the reflection of its surroundings. Facing Vesterbrogade, the ground floor of the building will contain shops and a café, and soon the streets surrounding the building will be given a makeover with wider pavements and new trees.

The building has gained 16,000 extra m², which include two totally new storeys facing *Rådhuspladsen* and three facing *Vesterbrogade*. A large atrium will face the *Tivoli* gardens. Its fan-shaped glass roof will slope down, in a sequence of steps, to a height of two storeys.

Axeltorv 2, København V   📍 D4

Rendering: Lundgaard & Tranberg Architects

👤 CLIENT	Ejendomsselskabet NORDEN
✎ ARCHITECT	Lundgaard & Tranberg Architects
🌾 LANDSCAPE	SLA
🔧 ENGINEER	COWI
📅 TIME	To be inaugurated in 2014

It is goodbye to Scala and hello to a completely new *Axeltorv* Square. There will be five new towers, an urban garden and green promenade, all of which will improve city life by providing the site with new recreational options. The green promenade is also a reference to Copenhagen's ramparts, which run like a historical thread beneath the city, where *Tivoli*, the Botanical Gardens and *Ørstedsparken* now stand.

Since the late 1800s, the site has been associated with leisure pursuits and amusements. First there was the concert hall and entertainment venue, 'National Scala', which kept the citizens of Copenhagen entertained right up until the 1950s. In 1957 National Scala was demolished to make way for the 'Anva' department store. The store closed in 1987 and the building underwent a radical renovation. In 1989, 'Scala' opened its doors with restaurants, shops, fitness centre, cinema and a basement discotheque. But, despite its central location and wide range of entertainment offerings, Scala struggled. Several subsequent attempts to breathe life into Scala failed, so the building was finally demolished.

The new building will consist of five tower-like constructions, placed asymmetrically and independent of each other. The five towers will be joined at the top by footbridges, so that at street level there will be free access between the buildings. The buildings will house a law firm, but the ground floor and first floor will be open to the public. There will be shops and restaurants and a public urban garden.

TRADE & INDUSTRY

106 CARLSBERG EXPERIENCE

Ny Carlsberg Vej 100, København V   📍 C5

👤 CLIENT	Carlsberg Group
✎ ARCHITECT	Ralph Appelbaum / PLH Arkitekter etc.
📅 TIME	To be inaugurated in 2016

In 1913 the brewer Carl Jacobsen donated the Little Mermaid to the people of Copenhagen. She was to become one of the city's major tourist attractions. The Carlsberg Brand and Experience Centre will represent Carlsberg's creation of yet another tourist attraction, which is expected to attract 400,000 visitors each year. The design of the winning project is the work of the American Ralph Appelbaum, the biggest designer of museums in the world, and PLH Arkitekter, an international team with just a touch of the Danish.

The brewery, which has over the years quenched thirsts with millions of litres of beer, and the iconic Elephant Gate, will provide the framework for the brand and experience centre. The actual conversion of the Elephant Gate and the brewery will accord with the mantra, KISS ('Keep It Super Simple'), and the beautiful old buildings will more or less remain as they are today. But when it comes to the contents, the keep it simple, sir philosophy goes out of the window. Everything inside is about entertainment. The focus will be on interactive experiences with the individual human being at the centre. In The Green Room digital ghosts will tell stories from Carlsberg's past, while a 'time machine' will transport visitors back to 1901, when the brewery was built. Then you can let off steam in four interactive rooms, each of which has its own theme (science, sport, music and art), and all of which offer various challenges, including dance competitions, mountain climbing and football matches. Finally you can enjoy a magnificent view of Copenhagen from the rooftop terrace, which will also serve as a bar, when darkness falls and the tourists have returned home.

SPINDERIET

Bomuldsgade 4, Valby B5

Photo: Jens Lindhe

👤 CLIENT	TK Development
✎ ARCHITECT	AK 83 Arkitekter
🔧 ENGINEER	Midtconsult
📅 TIME	Inaugurated in 2007

Until the mid-60s you could hear the whirring sound of *De Danske Bomuldsspinderier* ('The Danish Cotton Spinning Mills') here in Valby's old industrial district, where since 2007 the *Spinderiet* shopping centre has been housed. Unlike the large-scale proportions of traditional shopping centres, *Spinderiet* comprises a series of little lanes, which wrap around buildings, plazas and squares, both old and new. The lanes and plazas are covered by a 3-storey high glass roof, which guarantees both dry shoes and fresh air.

KPMG FLINTHOLM

Osvald Helmuths Vej 4, Frederiksberg B3

Photo: Adam Mørk

TRADE & INDUSTRY

👤 CLIENT	KPMG
✎ ARCHITECT	3XN
🌿 LANDSCAPE	Henrik Jørgensen Landskab
🔧 ENGINEER	MT Højgaard
📅 TIME	Inaugurated in 2012

Viewed from the air, the new headquarters of the accountancy firm, KPMG, resembles an angular three-leaved clover. Each of the three leaves houses an atrium and adjacent offices. The atria have been designed in a crystalline idiom with turquoise shades, but an elegant wooden floor lends some warmth to the somewhat arctic atmosphere. Futuristic footbridges, positioned at various levels, cross the atrium, providing connections between the offices. On the ground floor there are a number of business premises, which face the surrounding streets, making a contribution to urban life.

PATHS
& LINKS

Photo DISSING+WEITLING Next spread: Ty Stange

HELLE SØHOLT

CEO, Gehl Architects

"THE CITY IS A FINE MESH"

Photo: Marc Steffen Unger

In recent years the capital has invested considerable sums of money in paths, bridges, and other links, which have made it easier for vulnerable road users to move through the city, using new routes. "But the city's new links are much more than just routes to assist people in their journey from A to B," says Helle Søholt, CEO of Gehl Architects.

What significance do the new links have for the city?

"One of the major characteristics of Copenhagen, is the way the city is held together. The city is connected by a network, so you can pretty much get around everywhere on foot and by bicycle. In the last 10–15 years, the network has become even more sophisticated. Parks, squares and very small plazas on street corners are now included in a kind of single, vast, cohesive web that covers the whole city. In concrete terms, we move more freely through different areas of the city, which we might never have found it necessary to move around in before. Take, for example, the Green Cycle Routes. When you ride on them, you automatically cycle through both Nørrebro and Frederiksberg. In the olden days, many people regarded these two districts as entirely separate worlds. Today, they are united by a long green route.

Previously a link was a route that enabled you to get from point A to point B. It was pure necessity. But today what goes on between the two points is equally important. People commute by bike through residential areas, while residents use the area to pass the time in. This lends a whole new kind of dynamism and interaction to the city, which provides added value for all parties."

What trends are especially predominant?

"Health plays a very prominent role in the way we plan these links. Movement by bicycle or on foot throughout the city is high priority, and this encourages more people to walk or cycle. Along several stretches, there are also fixtures, playing fields, skating tracks or surfaces for roller skating, so every metre in a link is an invitation to physical movement.

Most recently, we have begun to focus on the activities which are a part of everyday life. When Copenhagen began working on its public spaces, it put the spotlight on

the entire event culture, and then on leisure. At that time the city was in the process of developing a new self-understanding as a sprawling metropolis. In recent years, everyday life with all its day-to-day, necessary activities has been much more integrated. Consideration should be given to how modern working patterns and family life (often with children from different marriages) can cohere. In this respect the links also possess an important economic significance for the city's infrastructure."

In your opinion, what should the priorities be for the future development of links?

"The links are all about the city as an organism, about our production, our transportation, our work and domestic lives. Many changes are occurring in those areas, and we can not fully predict the future. Therefore, I expect that we will need to develop several design solutions, which can change and adapt to the needs that will arise in the course of time. For example, one can imagine organising ourselves much more flexibly, so a motor traffic route could become a leisure area at weekends, then revert to its regular function from Monday to Friday."

What would you recommend people to go and see?

"I would recommend that you ride along the Green Cycle Route (112), starting from *Superkilen* (26) at Nørrebro and out to Frederiksberg. On this section, you get a very strong impression of city life in the many different neighbourhoods. which are situated from one end of the route to the other. Along the way, you will experience some of the very distinctive and diverse urban spaces which have been created in the capital over recent years. The bright red plaza at *Superkilen*, designed by BIG, is in all its rawness a very good example of an urban, highly diverse public space. At Frederiksberg you arrive at SLA's new squares (21) surrounding the metro station, *Frederiksberg Gymnasium* (82) and *CBS Kilen* (83). This is a completely different version of the city's diversity with its many vibrant promenades, water sculptures and atmospheric lighting in the evening. And from the start to finish of this route, you will encounter many examples of what a wonderful experience transport can be."

👤 CLIENT	City of Copenhagen	
✎ ARCHITECT	Inner Harbour Bridge:	
	Studio Bednarski / Canal Bridges:	
	Dietmar Feichtinger Architectes	
🔧 ENGINEER	Inner Harbour Bridge:	
	Flint & Neill / Canal Bridges:	
	WTM International Engineers	
📅 TIME	To be inaugurated in 2013	

When the 180-metre long Inner Harbour Bridge for pedestrians and cycles opens, Copenhagen will be united in a whole new way. The bridge will connect the city centre and Østerbro with *Amager* and *Christianshavn*, turning two of the city's main tourist areas, *Nyhavn* and *Christiania* into new neighbours. The bridge is also part of the 'Christianshavn Route', a bicycle route from the city centre through *Arsenaløen, Christiania* and *Kløvermarken*, leading cyclists from the city centre out into the countryside areas of *Amager*. The City of Copenhagen expects that between 3,000 and 7,000 cyclists will ride over the Inner Harbour Bridge every day.

The Inner Harbour Bridge is the first sliding bridge in Europe and thus adds a new type of bridge to Copenhagen's collection of swing bridges and bascule bridges. The bridge opens with the sections of the middle span being pulled horizontally away from each other to under the permanent spans. A sliding bridge such as the Inner Harbour Bridge is a major technical challenge, especially because the bridge is not symmetrical, but has a slight s-shape. This places great demands on both contractors and consultants, because all elements of the bridge must be consistent, right down to the last millimetre, in order to avoid uneven joints. On the other hand, a sliding bridge uses less energy than bascule bridges, because it is simply less energy-intensive to pull items away from one another than to hoist them into the air. The bridge will also be entirely illuminated with LED technology.

Renderings: Studio Bednarski / Dietmar Feichtinger Architects

The smaller Canal Bridges are bascule bridges with a minimalist appearance, which emphasises their functionality without attracting too much attention. In this way the appearance of the bridges is attuned to the specific cultural environment of which they become a part. The bridges relate, not only to the many listed buildings in the central harbour area, but also to the more noticeable architectural works such as the Opera House (03) and the Royal Danish Playhouse (02). The new bridges can all be opened up for sailing ships with masts, and their clearance height corresponds to that of existing canal bridges, thus accommodating everyday boat traffic.

The new bridges will undeniably form significant, new connections in the city. Although the Opera House was the prime reason for the new bridges, the more direct link to *Holmen* will be very important for the many students, who commute on a daily basis between *Holmen* and the inner city districts.

110 BRYGGEBROEN BRIDGE

Islands Brygge 32, København S

 D5

 Photo: DISSING+WEITLING

👤 CLIENT	City of Copenhagen
✏️ ARCHITECT	DISSING+WEITLING
🔧 ENGINEER	Carl Bro
📅 TIME	Inaugurated in 2006

When it was inaugurated in 2006, *Bryggebroen* became the first new bridge built across the harbour in 50 years. This 190-metre long bridge is exclusively for the use of cyclists and pedestrians, giving them a much needed short cut between *Islands Brygge* and *Kalvebod Brygge*. The spans can be swung to the side to open the bridge for passing ships. At night, fixtures in the bridge's railings create a band of light across the harbour and elegantly illuminate the bridge itself. From *Bryggebroen* there is a view over the whole harbour fairway, and you can easily sit down on the ridge, which separates bicycles from pedestrians.

111 ÅBUEN

Ågade 90, København N

 C3

 Photo: DISSING+WEITLING

 PATHS & LINKS

👤 CLIENT	City of Copenhagen / City of Frederiksberg
✏️ ARCHITECT	DISSING+WEITLING
🔧 ENGINEER	COWI
📅 TIME	Inaugurated in 2008

Ågade is one of the main thoroughfares into the city for motorists. For cyclists and pedestrians, on the other hand, it has always been a tough job to cross it. But, not only has the bridge changed this situation, it has gone even further. It is, in fact, a key component in the network of the city's Green Cycle Routes (112) and has now connected the entire stretch from *Nørrebro* to *Frederiksberg*, *Vesterbro* and *Valby*. The bridge has been commended for its elegance. Its curved, light shape makes it a small city gate, through which to enter the centre of Copenhagen.

Photos: Christian Bang

| 👤 CLIENT | City of Copenhagen /
City of Frederiksberg /
District Councils /
The Capital Region of Denmark |
| 📅 TIME | New routes are added regularly |

Copenhagen is one of Europe's most cycle friendly cities. In fact, every household in Copenhagen owns an average of two bicycles and the tradition for riding on two wheels is so strong, that one third of the city's daily commute consists of bicycles. In a massive effort to get more CO_2-neutral wheels turning, the City of Copenhagen has, from 2005–2013, invested almost DKK 900m in the city's network of cycle routes.

The strategy is straightforward: cycling should be fun and safe. The authorities seek to achieve this by leading cyclists along quick and interesting routes all over the city, through parks, across bridges and well away from motorists. The routes are planned simultaneously with the creation of more and more squares and plazas. That makes the routes part of the process, in which skaters, roller skaters and other wheels are also being given extra space, in areas such as Nørrebro Park and *Superkilen* (26). By 2025, the Green Cycle Routes will constitute a cohesive network totalling 110 km.

The goal is that, by 2015, half of the people of Copenhagen will be using the bicycle as one of their primary modes of transport. As a reinforcement of this idea, City of Copenhagen has entered into a partnership with more than 21 district councils and The Capital Region of Denmark to construct 28 bicycle super lanes, which will head out of Copenhagen and create a serious, comfortable and green alternative to car, bus and train. A total of 349 km of bicycle super lanes are planned. On cykelsuperstier.dk you can plan your route and calculate how much CO_2 you are saving. A mere 10 km saves 1.7 kg CO_2. That is not insignificant.

Photo: Kontraframe

CLIENT	Banestyrelsen / DSB
ARCHITECT	KHR Arkitekter
ENGINEER	COWI
TIME	Inaugurated in 2004

In 2005 a 120-year-old idea for a circle line in Copenhagen was realised. Today it is possible to get on the train in *Hellerup* and get off again 18 minutes later at *Ny Ellebjerg* at the other end of the city. *Flintholm Station* is the hub of the Circle Line. In next to no time it became the third busiest station in Denmark, after Copenhagen Central Station and *Nørreport Station* (117). The overriding idea was to bring together three stations in one, so regular trains, buses and metro trains depart from the same place, creating efficient transfers between the lines. Each of the three stations has its own individual space, while the station looks like a single harmonious whole.

Flintholm Station appears at once welcoming and strange. The station is flooded with light, because all the tracks run underneath a partition-less 5,000 m² glass roof. Regular or metro trains are constantly arriving at, or departing from the platforms, which are located at various levels. As opposed to the underground metro stations, the platforms at *Flintholm* are spacious enough to make waiting time pleasant for passengers. There is even a station café with tables and chairs right on the platform. *Flintholm* is also located in the middle of a park, which runs without a break beneath the station, adding a nice refreshing green touch.

METRO CITY RING

17 new stations in Copenhagen and Frederiksberg

Photos: Kontraframe

👤 CLIENT	Metroselskabet
✎ ARCHITECT	KHR Arkitekter
🔧 ENGINEER	Rambøll Atkins
📅 TIME	To be inaugurated in 2018

Between now and 2018 Copenhagen's metro will be extended with a whole new circle line, consisting of of 15.5 km and 17 stations. The City Ring's two new lines will encompass the existing metro like a giant ring. At the *Kongens Nytorv* and *Frederiksberg* metro stations passengers will be able to transfer between the city ring and the 'old' Metro. There will also be new metro stations at central hubs such as Copenhagen Central Station, City Hall Square, *Nørrebro Runddel* and *Trianglen*. The Copenhagen metro construction is divided into four phases, of which the City Ring is the fourth and provisionally the last.

The 17 new stations will be designed according to the same basic principles as the existing metro stations: large open spaces and easy access to the platforms. On the other hand. the stations will not all look the same. Wall coverings and platform surfaces, along with construction elements such as railings and escalators, will be designed in such a way, that the city ring stations will be more diverse to move around in. The forecourts in front of the stations will also have their own special character, tailored to the neighbourhoods they become a part of. This will be achieved by designing the distinctive skylights in different ways.

Construction of the City Ring also unearthed the largest archaeological site in Denmark. Archaeologists have been able to identify some new chapters in Copenhagen's history, including traces of a port at *Gammel Strand* in the 700s. This means that Copenhagen is now 300 years older than was previously believed.

PATHS & LINKS

CIRKELBROEN

Applebys Plads, København K ⬛ E4

Rendering: Olafur Eliasson

👤 CLIENT	Nordeafonden	
✎ ARTIST	Olafur Eliasson	
🔧 ENGINEER	Rambøll	
📅 TIME	To be inaugurated in 2013	

Cirkelbroen ('The Circle Bridge') over the Christianshavn Canal will establish a link between *Christiansbro*, on one side, and *Applebys Plads* and the harbour promenade at *Danisco*, on the other. It will make it possible to walk, jog or cycle all the way from *Islands Brygge* and up along the inner harbour.

The bridge consists of five overlapping circular decks of varying sizes, each with its own mast. The bridge was designed by the Danish-Icelandic artist Olafur Eliasson. Basing his concept on the history of *Christianshavn* and the culture around the canals, he used a ship as the visual starting point for the bridge. At first glance the bridge looks like a five-masted sailing ship moored across the outlet of the Christianshavn Canal.

Cirkelbroen has a clearance of 2.75 metres, allowing harbour cruises, kayaks and most motor boats to sail under without impediment. The bridge is also designed as a swing bridge. 2 of the 5 circles open like a garden gate in the Christianshavn Canal, so boats with masts can sail through, when necessary.

The bridge is not only intended as a connection, but actually creates a small plaza on the water. Rather than offering the fastest possible route over the canal, the bridge's sinuous path will encourage people to slow down and to gaze out over the water. This makes the bridge part of the City of Copenhagen's overall plan to encourage more people to stroll along the waterfront and to inject more life into previously unconnected areas of the city.

Rendering DISSING+WEITLING

👤 CLIENT	City of Copenhagen	
✎ ARCHITECT	DISSING+WEITLING	
🔧 ENGINEER	Rambøll	
📅 TIME	To be inaugurated in 2014	

The otherwise delightful bicycle ride across *Bryggebroen* Bridge (110), which connects *Islands Brygge* with *Vesterbro*, has for a long time been a source of vexation, because cyclists had to drag their bikes up and down a worn concrete staircase at *Dybbølsbro*.

To the joy of many cyclists, this annoying thorn in their bicycle tires has finally been extracted, and from 2014 they will be hurtling along *Cykelslangen* behind *Fisketorvet*, free of stairs, pedestrians and swimmers. This new connection will meander like a roller-coaster at a height of six metres above the water, from *Dybbølsbro* to *Havneholmen* (126), where some previously sharp corners will be rounded off.

Cykelslangen is the first bridge in the city for the exclusive use of cyclists, and is part of Copenhagen's ambition to be the best cycling city in the world. The bridge will be part of a larger network of bicycle connections, which, in addition to *Bryggebroen* Bridge, also includes the Green Cycle Routes (112) and *Åbuen* (111). The reorganisation of *Nørrebrogade*, which has resulted in fewer cars and wider bike paths, is another part of this strategy, and a similar initiative is planned for *Amagerbrogade*.

Together the links will create a traffic network for cyclists and pedestrians, which will make it possible to cross the city without car traffic. The number of accidents is expected to drop, and people will be exposed to less particle pollution. The future bridges in the inner harbour (109) and the planned expansion of the green land behind *Kalvebod Brygge* (128) will also become part of this bicycle network.

PATHS & LINKS

NØRREPORT STATION

Nørreport, København K

D3

👤 CLIENT	Banedanmark / DSB / City of Copenhagen
✒ ARCHITECT	COBE / Public Architects
🔧 ENGINEER	Grontmij / Rambøll
📅 TIME	To be inaugurated in 2015

It was never for fun that you turned up at the old *Nørreport Station*. You were bound to be standing in someone's way, the stairs looked like the set for a horror film, and it took forever to find your bike. But the rebuilding of *Nørreport* will make all these isues a thing of the past.

The new *Nørreport* is an open, cohesive space with clear and easily accessible facilities, created out of your very footsteps. A study of pedestrians' preferred routes at *Nørreport* was the actual basis for the design of the new station. Movement analysis showed how pedestrians move most naturally across the square, at the same time as identifying the areas, where there is not much traffic. Buildings, bicycle parking and other facilities are located organically, so that instead of creating obstacles,they generate a good flow across the square. The square is dominated by round shapes, which create a coherent look without 'back ends' or nooks and crannies. Bicycle parking is distributed over the entire square in small 'islands', which are sunken to a depth of 30–40 cm, so you are in no doubt as to where to park your bike

The new station buildings will be covered by one large organically shaped roof, which will unite the buildings and provide shelter from the elements. In the open areas there is space for street life, seating, shops and outdoor eating. All bus and car traffic is concentrated on the *Nørrebro* side, so the open space can flow naturally over into the pedestrian streets of *Fiolstræde* and *Købmagergade* (118).

Photo: Ty Stange

👤 CLIENT	City of Copenhagen
✎ ARCHITECT	KBP.EU – Karres en Brands & POLYFORM
🔧 ENGINEER	Oluf Jørgensen Ingeniører
📅 TIME	Inaugurated in 2013

Købmagergade is one of Copenhagen's busiest shopping streets, and for a long time its shabby pavement has been the city's guilty conscience. There was a time, when stiletto-heeled ladies from all over the world, shuffling teenagers and people with walking difficulties could easily fall on their face in the middle of rush hour, if a broken tile or patch of asphalt happened to be poking up in their path. This kind of discomfort will soon be a thing of the past, when the whole of *Købmagergade*, including *Kultorvet* and *Trinitatis Kirkeplads* at the Round Tower, is given a new, seamless paving, which will allow the flow of people to move freely from shop to shop.

The route starts at *Nørreport Station* (117), where the granite stone of the pavement is completely light in colour. As one moves down towards *Kultorvet*, the stone gets darker, and finally on Kultorvet the pavement is completely dark. At *Trinitatis Kirkeplads* the colour changes once again from light to dark. So the stones help to highlight differences in the urban space: not with changes in levels and types of stone, but with a graphic colour coding in smooth transitions. Trinitatis Kirkeplads has been fitted with LED lights in the pavement, an artificial starry sky on earth in recollection of the former observatory in the Round Tower.

Kultorvet's paving also refers to the past. Here the paving changes to a more serious character as a reference to the original trade in coal. *Hauser Plads* (37), above the Cleaning Facilities Centre (102) is also included in the project. Here there is a completely different atmosphere: a green oasis with a playground provides a bit of peace in the middle of the commercial hustle and bustle.

MASTER
PLANS

130

JENS KRAMER MIKKELSEN

CEO, CPH City & Port Development

"IF WE DICTATE EVERY SINGLE DETAIL, WE STIFLE CREATIVITY"

The past twenty years have witnessed a development of urban areas like never before in the history of Copenhagen. Jens Kramer Mikkelsen is the CEO of CPH City & Port Development, which has been involved in most of this development. He believes that politicians and planners should not have the power to dictate every detail of a plan.

What is so special about the way in which Copenhagen has grown in recent years?

"20 years ago, no one dreamed that Copenhagen would grow so rapidly. Today we have experienced urban development in the old industrial areas, in Ørestad (137), *Nordhavn* (119), and *Carlsberg* (125). What is particularly exciting is, that the city has grown within the city, instead of spreading out through the rest of Zealand. This has enabled us to develop more sustainable solutions for the city, and to focus on the qualities of the urban life, which we began to demand a decade ago."

What are the strongest trends in the way the city is being developed today?

"Sustainability, diversity, good public spaces, the use of water in the harbour and the green expanses of *Ørestad* have been essential values in the development of recent years. In the public debate one can occasionally get the impression that we have reached the highest level of human capability, in terms of urban development. We have not, and we never will. Society is changing, and we may need something completely different in just five years' time. This realisation is crucial to the way we build cities. Plans must be so robust that they can deal with the unpredictable. In my opinion it means that it is not the planners and politicians who should dictate every little detail. If we let them, we stifle the creativity which architects supply. A good example is *Tietgenkollegiet* (64) in Ørestad North. No circular building for the site figured in the master plan. The architects recognised the possibility, and today the building works fantastically in that very same place. There are also advocates for very strict local plans in the city. That is not my cup of tea. We cannot secure the future of the city simply by basing our plans on the requirements we recognise here and now."

Particularly in recent years, we have recognized that the city changes in stages. There may be periods, in which buildings will be smaller, or in which people are still in the process of establishing themselves in the new area. In these cases temporariness is a good resource. Temporary places can function for a period of time and help to engender new traditions, generating the life that might arise, when there are enough people. PLUG N PLAY (29) in *Ørestad* is an example of this way of thinking. It can be taken down and built up somewhere else, leaving space for another kind of life, which might occur later. Temporariness provides a constructive response to what needs to be done while we build cities."

What challenges face the development of the city in the future?

"We obviously have to continue to develop sustainable solutions. I also think we must cultivate and respect the diversity of the city far more than we do now. Everything should not resemble *Vesterbro* or *Christianshavn*, and there should not be sunshine and roses everywhere. The larger and more compact the city becomes, the more important breaks become, as an alternative to cafés and galleries on every street corner. There should be places for people who like *Ørestad*, yet there must also be places for people who like *Sluseholmen* (130) or *Vesterbro*. The city must make room for everything. Also in mental terms. Not everyone should like everything to the same degree."

What would you recommend people to go and see?

"I would suggest an excursion right out to the end of *Ørestad South* on the border between the city and countryside. It is a fantastic place with a strong contrast between the man-made and the natural. And go to *Sluseholmen*. If you stand at the point where the canal moves through the residential area, you can see all the contrasts. There is a transition between the harbour and the man-made channels, between the little red sheds of the boat club and the new apartments behind. Finally, I would recommend a walk out to the tip of *Nordhavn* to see how we are reclaiming land to expand the city."

MASTER PLANS

CLIENT	City of Copenhagen / CPH City & Port Development
ARCHITECT	COBE / SLETH / POLYFORM
ENGINEER	Rambøll
TIME	Work began in 2009

Probably the most ambitious metropolitan development project in Scandinavia for years to come, *Nordhavn* brings every lesson learnt from urban development during the last decade into play. The aspirations are soaring; the *Nordhavn* project will exhibit the sustainable city of the future for the world to see. Old factories, a cruise ship terminal, fishing port, cultural scene and a container harbour will be transformed into a new neighbourhood of 40,000 citizens and an equal number of workplaces.

Within a field of 180 Danish and international entrants, a young team of Danish architects won the competition for the plan. The main concept of their winning proposal is to transform *Nordhavn* into 11 separate islands with a variety of distinctive identities. Separated by canals, the focus of the islands will be to provide access to the harbour front – or even onto the water itself. The purpose of the divisions between the islands is to ensure the availability of a long and varied shoreline, whilst also improving the possibilities of water activities like kayaking and sailing.

The *Århusgade* district, situated closest to existing *Østerbro*, is currently being developed and realized. The area will accommodate nearly 1,700 residential buildings and 7,000 workplaces, basing its identity on the harbour area characteristics of simple infrastructure, storehouses and silos.

Over the years to come, a gigantic expansion will take place along the northeastern corner of *Nordhavn*. This is done in part to make room for a 1,100 meter wide

Renderings: COBE / SLETH / POLYFORM / Rambøll

cruise ship terminal, providing moorage for as many as three large cruise ships simultaneously. The soil stems partly from the excavation of the Metro City Ring (114). Providing the current supply of soil, the land gain will be completed in 2025 – expanding the Nordhavn area by nearly 1 mil. m².

The plan is to give the inhabitants the opportunity of feeling like urban dwellers while at the same time being close to nature, light, air and water. The city infrastructure of Nordhavn means that you can access the closest metro station, shopping facilities, workplaces and institutions within 5–10 minutes. Infrastructure is based on the principle af vulnerable road users with motorist priorities valued second. Being a dense city means that people and activities are concentrated in a small area, hereby reducing the transport emissions by making it easy to walk, bike or use public transport.

MASTER PLANS

120 AMERIKA PLADS

Amerika Plads, København Ø   📍 E2

👤 CLIENT   TK Development /
               CPH City & Port Development
✎ ARCHITECT   West 8
📅 TIME   Work began in 2000

Here the buildings are closer together and higher than the city is used to, and there is an international feel to the place. The Dutch firm of architects, West 8, based the project on the concept of creating a dense urban environment, characterised by large building complexes. *Fyrtårnet* (52) and *Kobbertårnet* represent two distinctive landmarks in the district. For some time *Amerika Plads has been* separated from *Østerbro* by railway lines and traffic. With the expansion of *Marmormolen* (121) and *Nordhavn* (119) the future will see a distinct improvement in terms of access.

121 MARMORMOLEN

Marmormolen, København Ø   📍 E2

👤 CLIENT   CPH City & Port Development /
               SNS Property Finance / Nordkranen
✎ ARCHITECT   3XN / Schønherr
📅 TIME   Work began in 2010

The tip of *Langelinie* and *Marmormolen* together make up the entrance for the Oslo ferry. In the future, the ferry will sail under a magnificent building, which will serve as a bridge to connect the two tips of the piers. The internationally renowned architect, Steven Holl has designed the LM Project, which will have a public walkway on the 17th floor. The star-shaped UN City (99) is also located here. The whole area is being transformed with canals and peninsulas, which will provide future residents, workers and visitors with direct access to the water.

MASTER PLANS

Rendering: TREDJE NATUR

👤 CLIENT	City of Copenhagen	
✎ ARCHITECT	TREDJE NATUR	
📅 TIME	To be inaugurated in 2016	

From now until 2016 the *Skt. Kjelds* district in *Østerbro* will undergo a total renewal. Multiple initiatives will make the neighbourhood more attractive and vibrant, in a process similar to that implemented in other areas, such as *Haraldsgade* in *Nørrebro* and the *Sundholmskvarteret* (136) on *Amager*.

One of several focus areas is climate adaptation, and the *Skt. Kjelds* district has been designated as an example project by the City of Copenhagen, who will transform this heavily asphalted district into the city's first 'Climate Neighbourhood', making it a flagship for this kind of project. According to the plan, an almost wild natural landscape will invade the stone bridge, thus transforming the area into a unique piece of urban nature. The area under development is the stretch between *Kildevældsparken* and *Fælledparken* (20), which includes *Bryggervangen*, *Skt. Kjelds Plads, Tåsinge Plads* and the adjoining courtyards, which will be transformed over the next few years into a 'third condition', a hybrid landscape at the intersection of city and nature. The architects promise both sensory experiences and technical solutions.

Rainwater and the dreaded torrential rain storms play a crucial role in the project. One of the ideas is to create more green surfaces, which can direct water away from streets and sewers, while contributing to the recreational aspects of the public spaces. The rainwater will also create experiences and value: for example, in *Bryggervangen* an urban stream will flow abundantly after heavy rain. There will also be artificial puddles, where water will accumulate, and *Skt. Kjelds Plads* will be fitted with water atomisers, which will emit a mist of rain water out over the square.

MASTER PLANS

123 FLINTHOLM

Finsensvej / Flintholm Allé, Frederiksberg 📍 B3

👤 CLIENT   City of Frederiksberg /
MT Højgaard / JM Danmark /
Pension Danmark

✏️ ARCHITECT   Holscher Arkitekter

📅 TIME   Inaugurated in 2010

Flintholm is located between single-family housing neighbourhoods and traditional blocks of flats. It was, therefore, logical that *Flintholm's* new buildings should borrow from both houses and residential blocks. The new blocks vary from two to six storeys and open out on to a central town garden, which lends some green character to the otherwise highly urban space. Sheltered housing units for the elderly (46), supermarkets and student residences have also found a home in Flintholm, not to mention the KPMG headquarters (108) and *Flintholm Station* (113).

124 PORCELÆNSHAVEN

Smallegade / Søndre Fasanvej, Frederiksberg 📍 B4

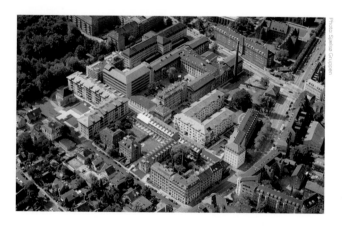

👤 CLIENT   Sjælsø Gruppen /
Dougthy Hanson & Co. /
European Real Estate Fund

✏️ ARCHITECT   Juul & Frost / Arkitema /
Henning Larsen Architects etc.

📅 TIME   Completed in 2007

Since 1882, the Royal Porcelain Factory has resided in *Frederiksberg*, but production has now moved. Many original buildings have been preserved and transformed in accordance with strict guidelines. Several high-ceilinged industrial buildings have been converted into studio apartments, while the neighbourhood has also been extended with a student hall of residence and a branch of the Copenhagen Business School. With reference to the old porcelain factory, the new housing projects have been given names such as 'Flora Danica Huset' and 'Fajancehaven'.

Carlsberg, København V   C5

👤 CLIENT	Carlsberg Ejendomme	
✎ ARCHITECT	Entasis	
🔧 ENGINEER	Esbensen Rådgivende Ingeniører	
📅 TIME	To be inaugurated in 2016	

In 2008 Carlsberg moved their production to *Fredericia*, after 160 years of brewing in the beautiful surroundings of Valby. They left behind a 330,000 m² area with unique historic buildings, parks and gardens, not to mention several kilometres of underground passageways. It will not be long before new sustainable buildings shoot up among the old listed buildings to create a whole new neighbourhood. More than 200 architectural firms from home and abroad entered the competition to create a new master plan for the area. The Danish practice Entasis won the competition with a plan for a densely constructed, sustainable neighbourhood with 16 different public spaces and an atmospheric synergy between new and old.

The goal is a relatively low and dense village, which will reduce and optimise the use of building materials. The buildings themselves will be energy systems. This will be accomplished mainly through effective insulation, energy efficient windows, heat recovery and implementation of renewable energy solutions such as solar heating, solar cells and wind energy. Building will comprise a total of 567,000 m², divided into 45 pct. for housing, 45 pct. for offices and shops, and 10 pct. for culture, sport and institutions.

The area, which was closed to the public, is now open to everyone with a view to generating life and activity even before construction starts. Several warehouses have been made available for artists, dance stages and galleries have been established, and several of the area's open plazas have been turned into temporary public spaces: for example, *Tap E Plads, Bobleplads,* and *Rebskoven.*

MASTER PLANS

126 HAVNEHOLMEN

Havneholmen, København V

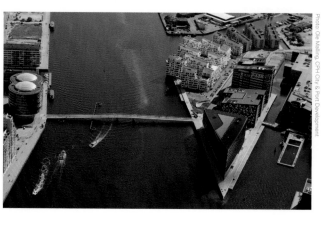

Photo Ole Malling, CPH City & Port Development

👤 **CLIENT** CPH City & Port Development /
Skanska / Sjælsø Gruppen /
Arp-Hansen Hotel Group

✎ **ARCHITECT** Wingård Arkitektkontor /
Schønherr

📅 **TIME** Inaugurated in 2010

The sloping roofs of the commercial and residential buildings, which surround the square where *Bryggebroen* (110) lands, form a bowl-shaped public space on the edge of the harbour. Particularly interesting are Lundgaard & Tranberg's residences (57) and *Allerhuset* (89), which sits enthroned on the triangular pier. *Havneholmen* is united by a promenade, which meanders in and out between the houses and gives passers-by access to the water. Very soon the *Cykelslangen* (116) will make its appearance, allowing pedestrians and cyclists to move with less friction.

127 ENGHAVE BRYGGE

Enghave Brygge, København SV

📍 D6

Rendering Juul I Frost Arkitekter

👤 **CLIENT** Nordicom / JM Danmark /
CPH City & Port Development

✎ **ARCHITECT** Gröning Arkitekter /
Danielsen Architecture /
Juul I Frost Arkitekter

📅 **TIME** Work begins in 2014

The iconic *H.C. Ørstedsværk* power station is to become the centre of a new district on *Enghave Brygge*. In the years to come, 300,000 m² of residential and commercial properties will be built on some of the last undeveloped land along the harbour. The neighbourhood will consist of 11 city blocks, of which 9 will be placed on separate islands along the pier. 35,000 m² of new land will be obtained of new land will be obtained, though some of this will be dredged and reduced by 30,000 m².

KALVEBOD BRYGGE

Kalvebod Brygge, København V 📍 D5

128

Rendering: Lundgaard & Tranberg Architects

👤 CLIENT   SEB / City of Copenhagen /
                 DSB Ejendomme

✏️ ARCHITECT   SLA

📅 TIME   Phase 1 inaugurated in 2010

It is no exaggeration to say that SEB Bank & Pension's new headquarters (85) on *Kalvebod Brygge* introduced a whole new perspective on commercial buildings in Copenhagen. In an unconventional way, buildings and landscape have been conceived as a total experience. The organic buildings seem almost to grow out of the constructed landscape, which rises above street level from the entrance on *Bernstorffsgade*.

The public are invited into the elongated park area, a piece of artificial Swedish landscape tucked away in the former railway facilities between waterfront office buildings and the new National Archives (71). Presently this green artery comes to a dead end at the *Tivoli Hotel*, but a new local plan, approved in 2012, will now make it possible to realise the architects' original dream and let the landscape continue all the way to *Dybbølsbro*. From there it will fall again and move south to *Otto Busses Vej*. In the nerve centre, which occurs around *Dybbølsbro*, relatively tall buildings will be constructed, so the isolated *Fisketorvet* will have more urban surroundings to nestle in. From there cyclists will soon be able to free wheel on the *Cykelslangen* (116) and continue across the harbour to *Islands Brygge*.

Today *Kalvebod Brygge* West is intersected by access roads and railway lines, but plans will invest this unpopular area with completely new qualities, making it a recreational link between a number of badly integrated areas. To the south, the link will provide access to the new neighbourhoods on *Teglholmen* (129) and *Sluseholmen* (130) and integrate them more successfully into the surrounding city.

MASTER PLANS

Photo: Kontraframe

👤 **CLIENT**   CPH City & Port Development / Sjælsø Gruppen / Nordicom / Skanska / Lawyer Allan Glud

✏️ **ARCHITECT**   Soeters Van Eldonk Ponec Architecten / Arkitema

📅 **TIME**   Under construction

Teglholmen is still a large urban development area at the southern-most end of the harbour. Along with *Sluseholmen*, *Enghave Brygge* and *Havneholmen*, it is part of the development plans for the area stretching from the south west of Copenhagen to *Vesterbro*. *Teglholmen* is still unfamiliar to many people, but the area has plenty of potential to develop into a delightful oasis on the fringe of the city. *Teglholmen* is already the location for a number of residential properties, including the interesting *Sømærk* (58), designed by *Tegnestuen Vandkunsten*. More developments are in the pipeline. On the eastern side towards the harbour a new canal village like the one at *Sluseholmen* will be built. The area's old industrial buildings will gradually be replaced or converted into a total of 5,000 dwellings, along with childcare centres and business facilities. Construction of a long-expected state school, *Sydhavn School* (69), will make the area more attractive for families.

Although, in 2011, *Teglholmen* was linked to *Sluseholmen* by a road bridge, it is still relatively difficult to access. However, a number of initiatives are planned to remedy this situation. A green boulevard will connect *Teglholmen* with the old residential area of *Sydhavnen* further inland. There are also plans for a footbridge across the harbour fairway to *Amager*. A new road bridge will link *Teglholmen* to *Enghave Brygge*, while the new development plans for *Kalvebod Brygge* (128) will connect *Teglholmen* with *Vesterbro*.

Teglholmen takes its name from the *Frederiksholm Tegl- og Kalkfabrikker* brickworks, who owned a big clay quarry on the site until 1908.

Sluseholmen, København SV   D6

Photo: Kontraframe

👤 CLIENT	City of Copenhagen / CPH City & Port Development
✎ ARCHITECT	Arkitema / Soeters Van Eldonk Ponec Architecten / Gröning Arkitekter
🔧 ENGINEER	COWI
📅 TIME	Inaugurated in 2007

Sluseholmen is located in the southernmost part of Copenhagen and is a vivid example of how industry in many places has left the harbour, thus freeing it to be incorporated into the everyday life of the city. *Sluseholmen* has been constructed as a completely new and densely populated residential area with space for business at street level, so that city life will gradually develop. Inspired by Java Island in Amsterdam, the Dutch architect, Sjoerd Soeters and the Danish firm, Arkitema created the overall plan for the area in association with the City of Copenhagen. This small canal village has been built in blocks around half open courtyards, and most buildings have direct access to the water, where bridges, wharfs and steps provide close contact with the water level. A number of different architectural practices have helped with the design of the multifarious façade, a process, which has not only enriched the place with detail and diversity, but has also been criticized for making the place look too theatrical.

On the other hand, there is nothing theatrical about the preserved Valby Boating Club, whose seafaring atmosphere and red boat sheds invest the neighbourhood with local colour. The ultimate contrast to this is the futuristic housing development *Metropolis* (59), built as a landmark on the northernmost point. In 2012 Copenhagen opened its third harbour swimming baths in Sluseholmen – *Koralbadet*. Both *Metropolis* and *Koralbadet* were designed by the architectural firm, Danielsen Architecture. In 2011 *Teglværksbro* bridge connected *Sluseholmen* with the rest of the city via *Teglholmen* (129).

MASTER PLANS

MARGRETHEHOLM

Approach from Refshalevej, København K

F3

👤 CLIENT	Sjælsø Gruppen
✎ ARCHITECT	Tegnestuen Vandkunsten
🔧 ENGINEER	Grontmij
📅 TIME	Work began in 2011

The wild area behind *Christiania* and *Holmen* (132) is now being transformed into yet another new neighbourhood. The new *Margretheholm* will be green and densely built up, and much of the existing vegetation will be retained and supplemented with avenue trees. Two different types of building will be constructed on the site. The town houses will have a dense, low and labyrinthine setting, while *Udsigten* ('The Prospect'), an eight-storey high building, will serve as the dramatic contrast and screen off the area from the dominant industrial plants in the east.

HOLMEN

Holmen, København K

F3

👤 CLIENT	NCC / 2L Development / Ministry of Culture etc.
✎ ARCHITECT	Henning Larsen Architects / Tegnestuen Vandkunsten etc.
📅 TIME	Work began in 1993

When the Danish navy moved from *Holmen* in 1993, a new neighbourhood was created, which also became home to a number of artistic educational institutions. Many of the old shipyards, sheds, forges and halls have been recycled in the formation of this new district. The empty lawns around the Opera House (03) have inspired dreams of both housing, which would create activity on the site, and the installation of a sound park, where opera music would be broadcast for everyone to hear. With the long-awaited Inner Harbour Bridges (109), *Holmen* will finally be united with the rest of the city.

MASTER PLANS

HAVNESTAD

Islands Brygge, København S   📍 D5   **133**

👤 CLIENT	JM Danmark / Sjælsø / NCC
✎ ARCHITECT	PLH Arkitekter / Tage Lyneborg / Dybroe & Hæstrup
📅 TIME	Completed in 2008

The first new residential area in the harbour is also the most criticised. The huge soya bean cake factory stood on the site up until 1991, when it thundered to the point of explosion. So the silence and purity of the new district with its tower blocks is particularly distinctive. Most buildings are residences with just a touch of business and a green belt that leads out on to *Fælleden*. One of the major criticisms levelled at the area is its lack of city life. In the opinion of most people, the explanation is that no space was made available for shops.

NØRRE CAMPUS

Tagensvej / Jagtvej / Nørre Allé, København N   📍 D2   **134**

👤 CLIENT	Universitets- og Bygningsstyrelsen
✎ ARCHITECT	COBE
📅 TIME	Work began in 2010

The plan is to transform the area, which is home to the faculties of health and science and situated next door to *Fælledparken* and the University Hospital, into a coherent modern science park. This new campus is being designed to strengthen the synergy between city, business and university. COBE won the competition for a master plan for the 418-acre area with a proposal, which will include increased access between the various areas of the campus. This will be implemented by the establishment of an extensive network of bicycle paths, crossing the major roads and boulevards, which today make it difficult to move from one area of the campus to another.

MASTER PLANS

135 THE MEATPACKING DISTRICT

Halmtorvet / Ingerslevsgade, København V 📍 D5

Photo: Kontraframe

👤 CLIENT   City of Copenhagen
✎ ARCHITECT   MUTOPIA
📅 TIME   Work began in 2006

When the city's creative brigade knocked on the door with a wish to use the location, the City of Copenhagen woke up to the fact that the white functionalistic concrete buildings, designed by the architect Poul Holsøe in the 1930s, might appeal to other people, as well as butchers. Today some of the city's trendiest galleries, restaurants and bars are found in the Meatpacking District, and many creative companies have moved into the rough rental units, all of which are listed and still in possession of their original character. The contrast between art and meat initially created some conflicts, but today no one faction can imagine the place without the other.

136 THE SUNDHOLM DISTRICT

Amagerbrogade / Amagerfælledvej, København S 📍 F5

Photo: Sundholmskvarterets Områdeløft

👤 CLIENT   City of Copenhagen
✎ ARCHITECT   GHB Landskabsarkitekter
👥 CONSULTING   Via Trafik / Orbicon
📅 TIME   To be inaugurated in 2013

Citizen involvement, sustainability and urban life are keywords in the makeover of the *Sundholm* district on *Amager*, which will be revitalised and become more attractive to move around and live in. For example, the residents' desire for green spaces, more street lighting and activities for young people in the neighbourhood have been integrated into the plans for the area's makeover. Concrete projects include *Tidselruten*, an eventful loophole with art and flowers, and the school yard at *Amager Fælled* School, which is being converted into an open city park which can also be used after school hours.

	CLIENT	CPH City & Port Development / NCC
✎	ARCHITECT	ARKKI
📅	TIME	Under construction

To date *Ørestad* is the biggest overall city development project in the history of Copenhagen. A considerable area of the countryside area of *Amager Fælled* was incorporated into the city, partly because the population was growing, and partly because the city was about to start building the Metro. The profits from the sale of the lots in *Ørestad* were used to finance part of the extensive metro construction. Roughly speaking, three new districts have come into existence: Ørestad North, Ørestad City and Ørestad South, each designed according to its own special principles. A total of about 8,000 people live in *Ørestad*, while 12,000 work there and about 20,000 go to school or university there.

The closest neighbour to the old Copenhagen is Ørestad North, created with the ambition of giving the city a new centre for culture, media and information technology, a logical idea, given the University of Copenhagen's location in the area. The IT University (67), *Bikuben Kollegiet* (63), *Tietgenkollegiet* (64) and the new *DR Byen* (01) have brought special life to this still fledgling district, the most built-up part of *Ørestad*.

The development of Ørestad City has been much more of an effort. The starting point here was virtually a bare field. For some years the *Fields* shopping mall has had a monopoly on shopping, but now delicatessens, cafés and supermarkets have started to ooze around the district's new architecture, of which VM Houses (42) and VM Mountain (41) are the iconic spearheads.

Furthest out is Ørestad South. Here new architecture, such as 8House (40), the upcoming Copenhagen Arena (16) and the temporary PLUG N PLAY (29), share the space at *Ørestad's* outermost tip with grazing cows. Rather unique for a city.

INDEX BY THEME
PAGE NUMBERS
& MAP COORDINATES